READY**SET**
KNIT CABLES

LEARN TO KNIT WITH **20** DESIGNS AND TEN PROJECTS

CARRI HAMMETT

Creative Publishing
international

Copyright 2007
Creative Publishing international
18705 Lake Drive East • Chanhassen, Minnesota 55317
1-800-328-3895 • www.creativepub.com

President/CEO: Ken Fund
Vice President/Sales & Marketing: Peter Ackroyd
Publisher: Winnie Prentiss
Executive Managing Editor: Barbara Harold
Acquisition Editors: Linda Neubauer,
Deborah Cannarella
Production Managers: Laura Hokkanen, Linda Halls

Creative Director: Michele Lanci-Altomare
Senior Design Manager: Brad Springer
Design Managers: Jon Simpson, Mary Rohl
Director of Photography: Tim Himsel
Lead Photographer: Steve Galvin
Photo Coordinator: Joanne Wawra
Illustrator: Peggy Greig
Photographers: Rudy Calin, Andrea Rugg, Joel Schnell
Special thanks to Suz Gill, Becky Helbling, and
Robyn Lamb for helping knit some of the projects.

Library of Congress Cataloging-in-Publication Data
Hammett, Carri.
 Ready, set, knit cables : learn to cable with 20 designs and 10
projects / Carri Hammett.
    p. cm.
Includes index.
 ISBN-13: 978-1-58923-293-8 (soft cover)
 ISBN-10: 1-58923-293-3 (soft cover)
 1. Knitting--Patterns. I. Title.
 TT825.H25647 2007
 746.43'2041--dc22   2006100072

Printed in China:

10 9 8 7 6 5 4 3 2 1

Due to differing conditions, materials, and skill levels, the publisher and various manufacturers disclaim any liability for unsatisfactory results or injury due to improper use of tools, materials, or information in this publication.

CONTENTS

INTRODUCTION

You've learned to knit and now you're ready to try some new techniques. One of the most versatile skills you can learn is how to knit beautiful, dimensional designs called cables.

Cables have a wide range of complexity. You'll notice as you work through the book that some cables are very simple. For instance, the Basic Cable contains just one unique direction other than knit and purl. Others like the Irish Twist are combinations of several different cables.

In the Knitting Cables Section of this book you will learn the basic steps used to make a cable. These steps will be demonstrated with numerous photographs of cables in progress. You'll also find information about techniques such as increases and decreases.

The Stitch Legend on page 9, is a glossary of all the ways to cross or cable stitches. Each cable has a title, a unique symbol, and a set of directions. Keep in mind that a cable is more than just the row where the stitches are crossed. There are also rows before and after the actual cross that give the cable its unique look—that's what learn as you work through the 20 cable designs. The Stitch Legend provides the ing blocks while the cable designs provide the construction diagrams.

This book contains directions for 20 different cable designs. Each cable is presented in two ways. It is illustrated in a chart, showing just the stitches necessary to make one repeat of the cable design with a few edge stitches. In addition, each cable is used in a swatch to demonstrate how that cable can be repeated both horizontally and vertically. The directions for the swatches are written out row-by-row and also shown in a chart. By knitting each of the swatches, you will realize that there is no mystery to making a cable. The swatches provide knitting practice, stimulate your imagination, and when you're all done you could even sew them together to make an afghan!

In addition to the swatches, there are 10 fun and unique projects for you to make with your newfound cable expertise. The projects vary in complexity from a simple cabled scarf to an evening bag or a journal cover. The projects are created from a wide range of fibers and colors; some projects are made from two yarns combined together. I think you'll find the projects fun to knit as well as vibrant and exciting to look at.

Ready, set, let's cable!

Carri Hammett

Carri Hammett is the owner of Coldwater Collaborative, a gem of a yarn shop in Excelsior, Minnesota. She loves everything having to do with fiber—knitting, weaving and quilting. Carri uses her strong sense of color and creativity to inspire her customers and design unique, knitted creations. She is also the ...nor of Scarves and Shawls for Yarn Lovers.

Carri lives in Minnesota with her husband; she also has three kids who don't visit often enough. She loves to hear from readers. Send her an email at carri@coldwateryarn.com.

For any of the fabulous yarns used in these projects, visit Carri's shop or web site:
Coldwater Collaborative
347 Water Street • Excelsior, MN 55331
www.coldwateryarn.com

WHAT IS A CABLE?

You already know what a cable looks like. A group of stitches that looks like a plain rib suddenly twists and becomes more like a rope. Or, several groups of stitches cross over each other and look woven or even knotted. These are all cables. Many knitters are intimidated by cables but they shouldn't be—cables are easy to knit once you understand the basic technique. Quite simply, a cable is created by knitting groups of stitches out of order.

Imagine you have four stitches on your left needle that you are getting ready to knit. From right to left the stitches are numbered 1 through 4. As you are knitting, you take stitches 1 and 2 off your left needle to wait safely (without dropping!) and place them onto a cable needle. While those stitches are out of the way and on the cable needle, you knit stitches 3 and 4 from the left needle. Next, knit stitches 1 and 2 off the cable needle. What you've done is change the order in which two groups of stitches have been worked—stitches 3 and 4 first, followed by stitches 1 and 2.

Where you keep the stitches waiting on the cable needle determines the direction that the cable crosses. If you keep the cable needle in front of your work while you knit the next (out of order) stitches off the left needle, then the cable will cross in a left direction. Conversely, if you put the cable needle behind your work, then the cable will cross in a right direction.

In addition to the direction that a cable slants, it can vary in other ways.
- The number of stitches in a cable can vary from two to 12 or more. You can put as few as one stitch on the cable needle to as many as six or even eight.

- The number of rows that are worked between the cable crossing can vary. In a simple, classic, interpretation of a basic cable, the stitches and rows are balanced. For instance, a cable of eight stitches will cross every eighth row.

- A cable can go straight up and down on your knitting or it can travel— the entire cable can move—diagonally.

- In addition to trading places, knit stitches and purl stitches can change.

You don't need to be an expert knitter to master cables. To get started, you really only need to know how to knit and purl. It's helpful to understand some basic characteristics of cables.

- Usually, cables are created out of knit stitches with purl stitches on either side. Because the knit stitch is higher than its purled-stitch background, it accentuates the cable.

- Cables draw the knitting together from side to side.

- Cables add density and therefore warmth to your knitting.

- Expect to use more yarn to cover the same area with cables compared to basic stockinette stitch.

TOOLS

Cable needles are available in many shapes, materials, and sizes but they are all pointed on both ends. Some are straight with either a dip or a bump in the middle (even a short double pointed needle will do). Others have a short handle with a 'U' shape at the end, like a fish hook. Cable needles can be made from metal, plastic, or wood. In addition, cable needles come in several sizes based on the diameter of the needle. The bulkier the yarn, the bigger the cable needle you will need. However, your cable `needle should always be smaller in diameter than your knitting needle, otherwise you might stretch your stitches. The type you use is a personal choice. Try a few different needles; you'll soon decide which type you prefer.

LEFT = FRONT

RIGHT = BACK

Use a trick in order to commit this rule to memory (my trick involves politics).

CHARTS

A knitting chart is a graphic format used to visually represent each stitch in a piece of knitting. Each square on the chart represents one stitch and each line of squares represents one row of knitting. Symbols for knitting stitches or directions are placed inside of the squares. Think of the chart as a road map. If you need to know how to drive somewhere you can either look at a map (the chart) or read the written directions for each turn (just like row-by-row knitting directions).

Read the chart from the bottom to the top. The first row of your knitting is represented by the first row of squares on the bottom of the chart. The last row of knitting is represented by the squares on the top of the chart. Odd numbered rows are right side (RS) rows and even numbered rows are wrong side (WS) rows. Each row is read horizontally before progressing up to the next one. So far, pretty easy but now you need to pay attention. Right side rows on the chart are read horizontally from the right to the left. Wrong side rows on the chart are read horizontally from the left to the right. If you are making a piece of knitting comprised of six stitches and eight rows then you would read the chart as follows:

Starting at the bottom right corner, the numbers in the squares on each row represent the order in which the stitches are to be worked before progressing up to the next row. It helps to understand the exact meaning of right side and wrong side. The right side is the public side, what is seen on the outside of a garment. The wrong side is the private side, the side that is worn next to your body and not seen. Knitting charts depict the work from the right side, the outside of your work. All of the projects in this book are knit back and forth.

CHARTS FOR KNITTING in the round are always read from right to left for every row (that's because you are always working on the right side, the public side, of the knitting).

Row 8 (WS)	1	2	3	4	5	6	→	
	6	5	4	3	2	1		Row 7 (RS)
Row 6 (WS)	1	2	3	4	5	6		
	6	5	4	3	2	1		Row 5 (RS)
Row 4 (WS)	1	2	3	4	5	6		
	6	5	4	3	2	1		Row 3 (RS)
Row 2 (WS)	1	2	3	4	5	6		
	6	5	4	3	2	1		Row 1 (RS)

SYMBOLS

Symbols are placed into the squares on a chart to indicate how a stitch or group of stitches should be worked. As you know already, the majority of knitting is created by using either the knit stitch or the purl stitch. The gold standard of knitting patterns is the stockinette stitch, which is knit on the right side (RS) and purl on the wrong side (WS). The 'symbol' to represent a knit stitch on the right side is actually a blank box that looks like this: ☐ Remember that each square of a chart represents a single stitch. The blank box means to knit that particular stitch on the right side and purl it on the wrong side.

A chart to represent Stockinette Stitch looks like this:

The directions for the chart read as follows:

Row 1: Knit.

Row 2: Purl.

Rows 3 – 8: Repeat rows 1 – 2 (3 times more).

Row 8 (WS)
Row 7 (RS)
Row 6 (WS)
Row 5 (RS)
Row 4 (WS)
Row 3 (RS)
Row 2 (WS)
Row 1 (RS)

The symbol to represent a purl stitch is a horizontal line and it means purl on RS, knit on WS. ⊟

Combining the two symbols to make a rib results in this chart:

Directions

Row 1: K2, p2, k2, p2.

Row 2: K2, p2, k2, p2.

Rows 3 – 8: Repeat rows 1 – 2 (3 times more).

Some helpful information about using charts:

- Read all the directions and look at the entire chart before you start a project. The charts and directions are helpful companions. If you don't understand a step in the directions or an area on the chart, you can often figure it out by using the companion.

- Photocopy the chart and enlarge it.

- The cable symbols in this book are a different color but you might find it helpful to develop some other color keys to keep track of your knitting. For instance, highlight the wrong side rows, or the background stitches.

- Develop a system to keep track of the row you are working in the chart. Use removable highlighting tape, put tick marks next to the row in the chart, or move a ruler up the page. A row counter can also be helpful.

- Charts actually look very much like your knitting. The plain boxes mimic the flat aspect of a knit stitch while the horizontal line symbol for a purl looks very much like the horizontal bumps of an actual purl stitch. Likewise, you can easily detect the shape and size of a cable in the chart. Use this as another tool.

- Charts and knitting directions are not always perfect. Learn to think for yourself and be sure and let me know if you find a mistake.

The stitch legend on page 9 explains in detail what each symbol means. Mark this page in your book because you will refer to it often. Or make a photocopy of the page for easy reference.

STITCH LEGEND

 Knit on RS, purl on WS

 Purl on RS, knit on WS

 Make Bobble (MB) - (page 21)

 K2tog in knit stitches; P2tog in purl stitches

 SSK

○ Yarn Over (yo)

3-St RKC Slip next stitch to cable needle and hold at back of work, knit next 2 stitches from left needle, knit stitch from cable needle

3-St RPC Slip next stitch to cable needle and hold at back of work, knit next 2 stitches from left needle, purl stitch from cable needle

3-St LKC Slip next 2 stitches to cable needle and hold at front of work, knit next stitch from left needle, knit 2 stitches from cable needle

3-St LPC Slip next 2 stitches to cable needle and hold at front of work, purl next stitch from left needle, knit 2 stitches from cable needle

4-St RKC Slip next 2 stitches to cable needle and hold at back of work, knit next 2 stitches from left needle, knit 2 stitches from cable needle

 4-St RPC Slip next 2 stitches to cable needle and hold at back of work, knit next 2 stitches from left needle, purl 2 stitches from cable needle

 4-St LKC Slip next 2 stitches to cable needle and hold at front of work, knit next 2 stitches from left needle, knit 2 stitches from cable needle

 4-St LPC Slip next 2 stitches to cable needle and hold at front of work, purl next 2 stitches from left needle, knit 2 stitches from cable needle

 5-St RC Slip next 3 stitches to cable needle and hold at back of work, knit next 2 stitches from left needle, slip next stitch from cable needle back to left needle and purl it, knit remaining 2 stitches from cable needle

 5-St RPC Slip next 2 stitches to cable needle and hold at of back of work, knit next 3 stitches from left needle, purl 2 stitches from cable needle

 5-St LPC Slip next 3 stitches to cable needle and hold at front of work, purl next 2 stitches from left needle, knit 3 stitches from cable needle

 6-St RKC Slip next 3 stitches to cable needle and hold at back of work, knit next 3 stitches from left needle, knit 3 stitches from cable needle

 6-St LKC Slip next 3 stitches to cable needle and hold at front of work, knit next 3 stitches from left needle, knit 3 stitches from cable needle

 6-St RC Slip next 4 stitches to cable needle and hold at front of work, knit next 2 stitches from left needle, slip next 2 stitches from cable needle back to left needle, pass cable needle with remaining 2 sts to back of work, purl 2 sts from left needle, knit next 2 sts from cable needle

 7-St LKC Slip next 4 stitches to cable needle and hold at front of work, knit next 3 stitches from left needle, knit 4 stitches from cable needle

 8-St RKC Slip next 4 stitches to cable needle and hold at back of work, knit next 4 stitches from left needle, knit 4 stitches from cable needle

 8-St LKC Slip next 4 stitches to cable needle and hold at front of work, knit next 4 stitches from left needle, knit 4 stitches from cable needle

 8-St RIB RC Slip next 4 stitches to cable needle and hold at back of work, (k1, p1) twice from left needle, (k1, p1) twice from cable needle

 8-St RPC Slip next 4 stitches to cable needle and hold at back of work, purl next 4 stitches from left needle, knit 4 stitches from cable needle.

 8-St LPC Slip next 4 stitches to cable needle and hold at front of work, knit next 4 stitches from left needle, purl 4 stitches from cable needle.

 **9-St RKC** Slip next 4 stitches to cable needle and hold at back of work, knit next 5 stitches from left needle, knit 4 stitches from cable needle

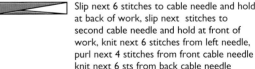 **16-St RC** Slip next 6 stitches to cable needle and hold at back of work, slip next stitches to second cable needle and hold at front of work, knit next 6 stitches from left needle, purl next 4 stitches from front cable needle knit next 6 sts from back cable needle

KNITTING CABLES

The variables in a cable are: the direction of the cross, the number of stitches involved, and whether the stitches are knit or a combination of knit and purl. The charts and directions below and on the next few pages explain all of these variables, from the easiest to more complex. The directions and photographs walk you through and show you how it's done. Grab some needles and medium-weight yarn, and practice these cable techniques.

FOUR-STITCH LEFT KNIT CROSS
4-ST LKC ▨▨

These simple cables are made exclusively from knit stitches and they travel straight up and down to form a twisted column or rope. One of the easiest cables to learn is a four-stitch cable that crosses every fourth row. The symbol looks like this ▨▨ and the abbreviation is 4-St LKC. There's a lot of information contained in the box with the blue symbol. The box is four squares wide (this is easy to tell when used in a grid) so you know the cable involves four stitches. The blue symbol inside the box makes an X. The heavier, unbroken line in front points to the upper left, which tells you that the cable will cross to the left. To make that happen, you will need to put the cable needle with the out of order stitches in the front of the knitting. The directions will say, "hold at front of work."

When working cables, there are usually several set-up rows before the cable begins. Work rows 1 and 2 of the pattern and repeat them a couple times. Then begin following the chart, beginning with row 1.

Cast on 12 stitches.
When working cables, there are usually several set-up rows before the cable begins. Work rows 1 and 2 of the pattern and repeat them a couple times. Then begin following the chart, beginning with row 1.
Row 1: P4, k4, p4.
Row 2: K4, p4, k4.
In a standard pattern, this is how the directions for Row 3 would appear:
Row 3: P4, 4-St LKC, p4.

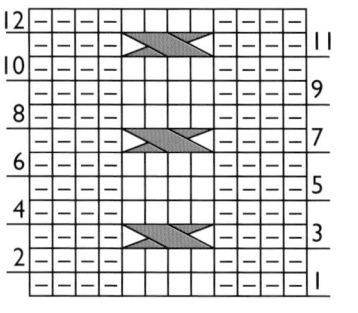

Here's what the directions mean:

1 Purl four stitches then move the working yarn to the back of your knitting as if you were getting ready to knit. Transfer the right needle to your left hand and hold it lightly behind the left needle so that you have easy access to the stitches on the left needle. With the cable needle in your right hand insert the left point of the cable needle into the front of the next two stitches on the left needle as if you were getting ready to purl them.

2 Slide these stitches off the left needle and onto the cable needle. You now have two stitches that should be resting in the middle section on the cable needle.

3 Drop the cable needle and just let it hang loosely, holding two stitches in the front of your knitting.

4 Put the right needle back into your right hand. Working behind the cable needle, knit the next two stitches on the left needle.

5 Tuck the left needle between your fingers so that you can hold the left needle and the cable needle at the same time.

6 Slide the two stitches that are waiting to the right side of the cable needle. Use the right needle to knit these two stitches off of the cable needle.

7 Complete the row by purling the last four stitches.

Row 4: K4, p4, k4.
Row 4 is identical to Row 2. Even though the middle stitches have a cable crossing, they are still knit stitches on the right side and purl stitches on the wrong side. They will feel tight and crowded but this is normal; purl the middle stitches just like you did on Row 2.

Row 5: P4, k4, p4.
Row 6: K4, p4, k4.
You have now added 3 rows of knitting after the first cable crossing. Since the cable is crossed every fourth row it's time to cross again. This is how the directions will appear in a standard pattern:

Row 7: P4, 4-St LKC, p4.
Row 8: K4, p4, k4.
Rows 9 – 12: Repeat rows 1 – 4.

You have just created a cable by knitting two groups of stitches out of order. You put two stitches on a cable needle to wait out of the way while you knit the next two stitches from the left needle. Then you pulled the two stitches that were waiting across the front by knitting them from the cable needle.

IT IS PERFECTLY normal, even expected, that your first attempts at creating cables will feel awkward and slow. You will wonder how you could possibly make an entire garment with cables if your first cable took five minutes. I promise that this will get easier. Besides, that's what the swatches in the book are for—practice!

FOUR-STITCH RIGHT KNIT CROSS
4-ST RKC

This cable is just like the first one except for the direction it crosses. The heavy, unbroken line of the X points to the right, so you put the cable needle with the held stitches behind the knitting, and the cable will cross to the right instead of the left.

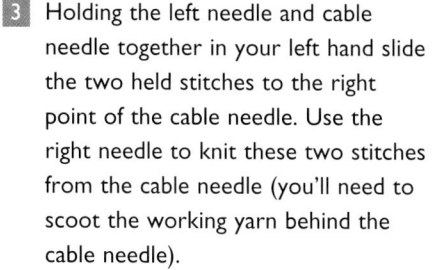

Cast on 12 stitches. Using the chart above, knit the first two rows as follows:

Row 1: P4, k4, p4.

Row 2: K4, p4, k4.

In a standard pattern, this is how the directions for Row 3 would appear:

Row 3: P4, 4-St RKC, p4.

Here's what the directions mean:

1. Purl the first four stitches. Leave the working yarn in front. Transfer the right needle to your left hand and hold the needles so that you have easy access to the stitches on the left needle. With the cable needle in your right hand, reach in from behind the knitting to transfer two stitches from the left needle to the cable needle. Make sure to insert the cable needle into the stitches as if you are getting ready to purl.

2. Drop the cable needle and allow it to hold the stitches behind your knitting. Now, move the working yarn behind the left needle to get ready to knit, but keep the yarn in front of the cable needle. With the right needle back in your right hand, knit the next two stitches from the left needle.

3. Holding the left needle and cable needle together in your left hand slide the two held stitches to the right point of the cable needle. Use the right needle to knit these two stitches from the cable needle (you'll need to scoot the working yarn behind the cable needle).

4. Complete the row by purling the last four stitches.

Now complete the chart.

Row 4: K4, p4, k4.

Row 5: P4, k4, p4.

Row 6: K4, p4, k4.

Row 7: P4, 4-St RKC, p4.

Row 8: K4, p4, k4.

Rows 9 – 12: Repeat rows 1 – 4.

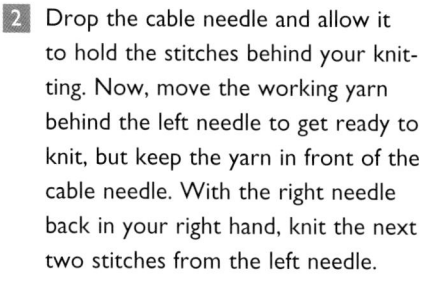

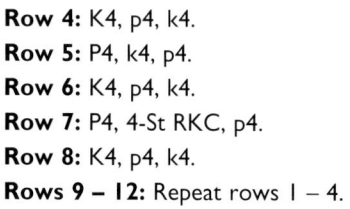

EIGHT-STITCH LEFT KNIT CROSS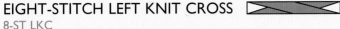
8-ST LKC

If the directions call for an 8-St LKC, you knit it just like a 4-St LKC except you cross four stitches in front instead of two stitches. Also, for a balanced cable, you will knit seven rows between cable crossings instead of three rows.

When you reach the cable row:

1 Knit to the location of the cable crossing and slip four stitches to the cable needle, inserting the cable needle into the stitches as if to purl. Hold the needle at front of work.

2 Knit four stitches from the left needle. Knit the held stitches from the cable needle. As you can see, this cable is exactly like the four-stitch version only it's wider.

THREE-STITCH LEFT KNIT CROSS
3-ST LKC

The numbers of stitches crossing do not need to be equal. For instance, you can make a three-stitch cable.

When you reach the cable row:

1 Slip next two stitches to the cable needle and hold at front of work.

2 Knit next stitch from left needle (just one stitch!).

3 Knit two stitches from cable needle.

THREE-STITCH RIGHT KNIT CROSS
3-ST RKC

When you reach the cable row:

1 Slip next stitch to cable needle (just one stitch) and hold at back of work.

2 Knit next two stitches from left needle.

3 Knit stitch from cable needle.

FOUR-STITCH LEFT PURL CROSS
4-ST LPC

You can also make cables that move diagonally across your knitting. For example, in the Irish Twist on page 64, a four-stitch cable splits into two smaller bands that diverge and then converge back in order to create a diamond filled with seed stitch. Remember that most cables are composed of knit stitches surrounded by a purl-stitch background. This type of cable is accomplished when the knit stitches and purl stitches trade places. These cables are called either a Left Purl Cross or a Right Purl Cross.

Just like Knit Crosses, Purl Crosses can be composed of an even or odd number of stitches. The specific directions in the Symbol Legend (page 9) will specify how many stitches to put on the cable needle and which order to knit and purl.

Notice that the symbol is different: the wide band in front, indicating the direction of the cable, is still blue but the two arms in back are grey. **When you see a bi-color cable symbol like this it means that purl stitches are involved.**

A sample chart for this type of diagonal cable looks a little different. In this case, a rib is going to move over four stitches to the left; the knit stitches are going to trade places with the purl stitches.

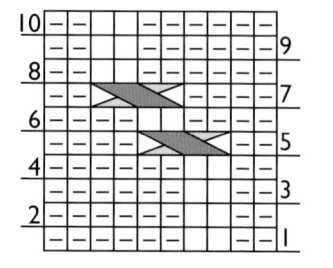

Cast on 10 stitches. Work the first four rows according to the chart.
In a standard pattern, this is how the directions for Row 5 would appear:
Row 5: P2, 4-St LPC, p4.

Here's what the directions mean:

1. Purl the first two stitches then slip the next two stitches to a cable needle and hold in front of your work. Here's where it gets tricky: purl the next two stitches from the left needle.

2. Knit the two stitches from the cable needle.

3. Purl the remaining four stitches in the row. The knit stitches have shifted two stitches to the left.

Row 6: K4, p2, k4. Be a little careful since the position of the knits and purls has changed.
Row 7: P4, 4-St LPC, p2. Work the cable just like row 5.

Work the last three rows according to the chart.

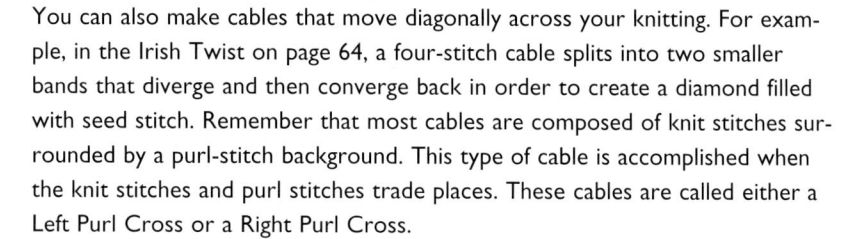

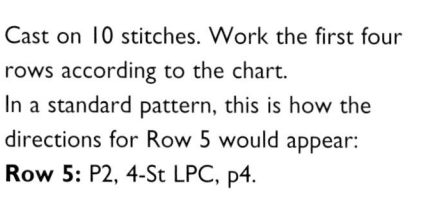

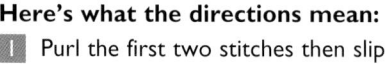

FOUR-STITCH LEFT PURL CROSS AND
FOUR-STITCH RIGHT PURL CROSS

4-ST LPC AND 4-ST RPC

Cables that travel diagonally can be combined to form honeycombs, diamonds, even X's and O's. Experiment by working this little chart.

Cast on 12 stitches.
Row 1: P4, k4, p4.
Row 2: K4, p4, k4.
Row 3: P2, 4-St RPC, 4-St LPC, p2.

Here's what the directions mean:

1. Purl two stitches. Slip the next two purl stitches to cable needle and hold in back of work.

2. Knit two stitches from left needle, then purl two stitches from cable needle to complete the 4-St RPC.

3. Slip the next two knit stitches to cable needle and hold in front. Purl the next two stitches from the left needle then knit the two stitches from the cable needle. You've shifted four purl stitches to the center of the cable.

For the next three rows, work the stitches in the new pattern that's been established.

Row 4: K2, p2, k4, p2, k2.
Row 5: P2, k2, p4, k2, p2.
Row 6: K2, p2, k4, p2, k2.
Row 7: P2, 4-St LPC, 4-St RPC, p2. This is the mirror image of row 4.

You will shift the purl stitches back to the outside of the cable—all the stitches are now in their original places.

Row 8: K4, p4, k4.

EIGHT-STITCH RIB RIGHT CROSS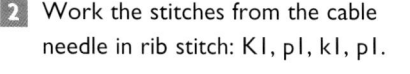
8-ST RIB RC

Sometimes, all the stitches in a cable are worked in rib stitch. This produces a reversible cable. To work this cable:

1 Slip 4 stitches on the cable needle and hold in back, just like a standard eight-stitch right cross. Work the next four stitches on the left needle in rib stitch: K1, p1, k1, p1.

2 Work the stitches from the cable needle in rib stitch: K1, p1, k1, p1.

3 Continue working both the wrong side and the right side of the cable stitches in rib stitch.

FIVE-STITCH RIGHT CROSS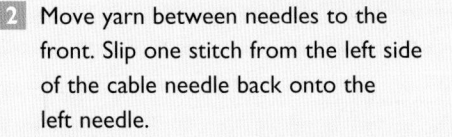
5-ST RC

Think of this cable as a four-stitch right knit cross with an extra purl stitch in the middle.

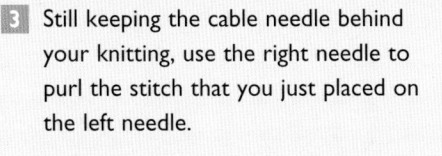

1 Slip three stitches to the cable needle and hold at the back of the work. Knit two stitches from the left needle (so far this is just like a 4-St RKC).

2 Move yarn between needles to the front. Slip one stitch from the left side of the cable needle back onto the left needle.

3 Still keeping the cable needle behind your knitting, use the right needle to purl the stitch that you just placed on the left needle.

4 Move yarn between the needles to the back. Knit the two stitches from the cable needle.

KNOTTED CABLES

There are two knotted cables used in this book. In both cases, purl stitches move straight up the work with knit stitches crossed behind. The purl stitches look like the knot that holds a bow together. Although the concept is the same for both cables they are accomplished differently.

SIX-STITCH RIGHT CROSS
6-ST RC

1. Slip four stitches to the cable needle and hold them in front—this breaks the rule because the cable is a right cross. You will move the cable needle behind after you use it to help make a knot. Knit two stitches from the left needle.

2. Slip two stitches from the left side of the cable needle back onto the left needle.

3. Pass the cable needle with the remaining two stitches between the needles to the back of your work.

4. Move the yarn between the needles to the front. Purl the next two stitches from the left needle.

5. Move the yarn between the needles to the back. Knit two stitches from the cable needle.

16-STITCH RIGHT CROSS

16-ST RC

To make this cable you will need two cable needles.

1 Slip six stitches to the first cable needle and hold the stitches at the back of your work. Slip four stitches onto a second cable needle and hold in front of your work—these are the stitches that will form the purl knot in front of the knit cross.

2 Knit six stitches from the left needle. This step will feel awkward because you are working between the two cable needles.

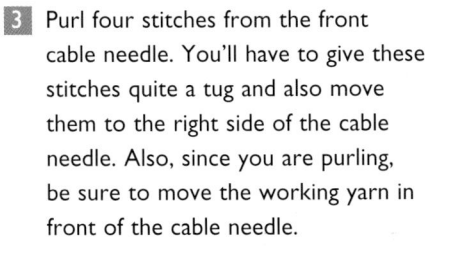

3 Purl four stitches from the front cable needle. You'll have to give these stitches quite a tug and also move them to the right side of the cable needle. Also, since you are purling, be sure to move the working yarn in front of the cable needle.

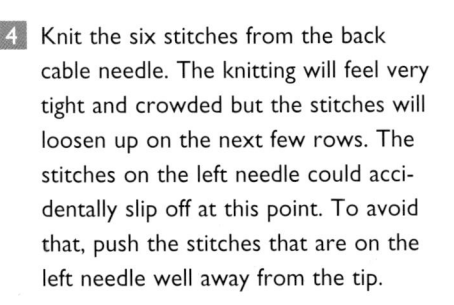

4 Knit the six stitches from the back cable needle. The knitting will feel very tight and crowded but the stitches will loosen up on the next few rows. The stitches on the left needle could accidentally slip off at this point. To avoid that, push the stitches that are on the left needle well away from the tip.

5 When you work the first wrong side row after the cable crossing it's difficult to distinguish the center stitches, which are to be knit (after being purled on the front side). Pay careful attention to the directions and chart for the wrong side rows, and don't forget to count!

ADDITIONAL TECHNIQUES

To make all the projects in this book you need to know a few techniques in addition to knit and purl.

INCREASE ONE STITCH
INC 1 ST

1 If increasing into a knit stitch, first knit in the usual way but don't take the new stitch off the needle. Pivot the right needle to the back of the left needle and insert it knitwise (from front to back) into the back loop of the same stitch you just worked. Make another knit stitch in the back loop.

Slip the old stitch off the left needle. Now you have two stitches in place of one.

2 If increasing into a purl stitch, first purl in the usual way but don't take the new stitch off the needle. Keeping the working yarn in front, pivot the right needle to the back of the left needle and insert it purlwise (from the back to the front) into the back loop of the same stitch you just worked.
Make another purl stitch in the back loop.

Slip the old stitch off the left needle. Now you have two stitches in place of one.

MAKE ONE INCREASE
M1

1 If you pull your knitting from side to side you'll notice that a little ladder is formed between the stitches. Insert your left needle from front to back under this ladder.

2 You now have a new loop on the left needle. To give this new stitch an extra twist, knit into the back loop (the loop furthest away from you).

19

KNIT TWO TOGETHER DECREASE ☒
OR PURL TWO TOGETHER DECREASE
K2TOG OR P2TOG

The symbol for this decrease is the same regardless of whether it is being worked into knit stitches or purl stitches. In either case you work two stitches at the same time.

K2tog: Insert the right needle knitwise (from front to back) into the next two stitches on the left needle. Knit these two stitches at the same time as if they were one stitch. You have just decreased by one stitch.

P2tog: Insert the right needle purlwise (from back to front) into the next two stitches on the left needle. Purl theses two stitches at the same time as if they were one stitch. You have just decreased by one stitch.

SLIP, SLIP, KNIT ☒
SSK

This decrease is very similar to a K2tog except that the decrease is knit through the back loops of two stitches at the same time. Working one at a time, slip two stitches to the right needle as if you were going to knit them (knitwise). Insert the tip of the left needle into the front loops of these two stitches.

YARN OVER ☐
YO

Wrap the yarn over the needle creating a loop that will be worked as a new stitch on the next row. The yarn over leaves a distinctive hole in your knitting and is often used decoratively. Yarn overs are worked differently depending on hether you are knitting or purling.

Knit: Bring the yarn forward and lay it over the right needle in a counterclockwise direction ending behind the two needles. Knit the next stitch. Notice that the yarn has made an extra loop on the needle.

Purl: Keeping the yarn in front, wrap it counter-clockwise around the right needle. Purl the next stitch. Notice that the yarn has make an extra loop on the needle.

Now your right needle is in the back loops of the two stitches that are being decreased. Knit these two stitches at the same time through the back loops as if they were one stitch. You have just decreased by one stitch.

MAKE BOBBLE ◉
MB

(K1, yo, k1, yo, k1) all into the next st, turn, purl 5, turn, knit 5, turn, p2tog, p1, p2tog, turn, slip 1, k2tog, pass slip st over.

Bobbles are created by 'stalling' on the stitch where you want the bobble to be. You increase many times into that single stitch and then knit back and forth on the newly created stitches. Finally, the bunch of stitches is decreased back to one stitch. Here's how:

1 Work up to the stitch where you want to place the bobble. Knit the stitch and draw the yarn through to the front but don't remove the stitch from the left needle.

2 Yarn over by moving the yarn forward between the two needles and then lay it over the right needle in a counter-clockwise direction.

3 Knit into the same left stitch again but still don't remove the stitch from the needle.

4 Work another yarn over. The last step is to knit one more time into the left stitch but this time remove the old stitch from the left needle. Notice that you have five new stitches coming out of the single stitch that you just took off the left needle.

5 Turn the knitting so that you are looking at the wrong side. Purl just the five new stitches.

   Turn the knitting again so you are looking at the right side. Knit the five loops.

6 Turn the knitting again and work some decreases as follows: purl 2 stitches together, purl 1 stitch, purl 2 stitches together.

7 Turn the knitting back to right side and work the last set of decreases as follows: slip 1 stitch to the right needle as if you were going to knit it, knit the next two stitches together, then pass the slipped stitch over the knit stitch and off the end of the right needle (just like binding the stitch off).

8 Continue across the row as directed in the pattern. When you reach the bobble stitch on the wrong side, work it as the single stitch shown in the chart but make it a very tight stitch.

BASIC CABLE

The basic cable is a building block for more complex cables. The number of stitches in a basic cable can vary from two to 12 or more. In addition, the number or rows that are worked in between the cable crossing can vary. In the most simple, yet classic, interpretation of a basic cable the stitches and rows are balanced. For instance, this cable is eight stitches wide and it is repeated every eight rows.

BASIC PATTERN
Multiple of 8 stitches with 4 edge stitches (optional)

RIGHT SLANTING CABLE
(8-ST RKC)
As shown on left side of swatch
Row 1 (RS): P2, k8, p2.
Row 2: K2, p8, k2.
Row 3: P2, 8-St RKC, p2.
Row 4: K2, p8, k2.
Row 5: P2, k8, p2.
Row 6: K2, p8, k2.
Row 7: P2, k8, p2.
Row 8: K2, p8, k2.
Repeat rows 1 – 8.

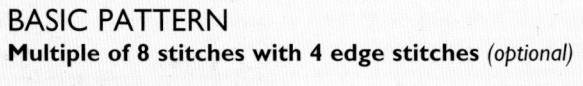

☐ Knit on RS, purl on WS
⊟ Purl on RS, knit on WS
8-St RKC

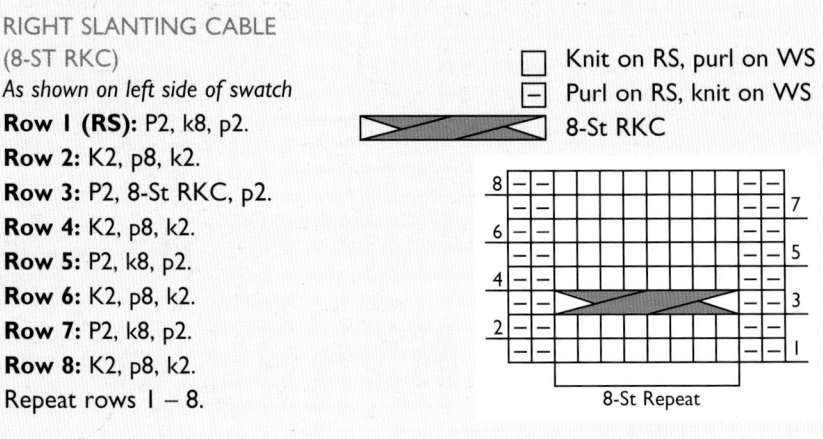

8-St Repeat

LEFT SLANTING CABLE
(8-ST LKC)
As shown on right side of swatch
Row 1 (RS): P2, k8, p2.
Row 2: K2, p8, k2.
Row 3: P2, 8-St LKC, p2.
Row 4: K2, p8, k2.
Row 5: P2, k8, p2.
Row 6: K2, p8, k2.
Row 7: P2, k8, p2.
Row 8: K2, p8, k2.
Repeat rows 1 – 8.

☐ Knit on RS, purl on WS
⊟ Purl on RS, knit on WS
8-St LKC

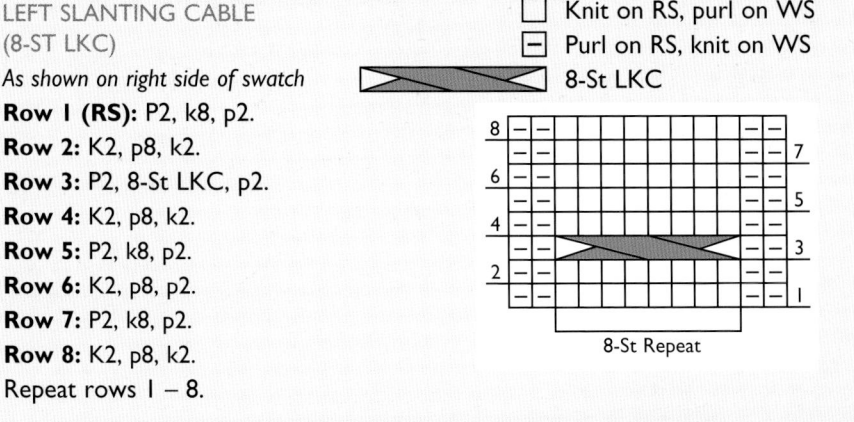

8-St Repeat

BASIC CABLE – MAKE A SWATCH

Cast on 32 stitches.

Row 1 (RS): K4, p2, k8, p4, k8, p2, k4.

Row 2: K6, p8, k4, p8, k6.

Row 3: K4, p2, k8, p4, k8, p2, k4.

Row 4: K6, p8, k4, p8, k6.

Row 5: K4, p2, k8, p4, k8, p2, k4.

Row 6: K6, p8, k4, p8, k6.

Row 7: K4, p2, 8-St LKC, p4, 8-St RKC, p2, k4.

Row 8: K6, p8, k4, p8, k6.

Rows 9 – 32: Repeat rows 1 – 8 (3 more times).

Row 33: K4, p2, k8, p4, k8, p2, k4.

Row 34: K6, p8, k4, p8, k6.

Row 35: K4, p2, k8, p4, k8, p2, k4.

Row 36: K6, p8, k4, p8, k6.

Row 37: K4, p2, k8, p4, k8, p2, k4.

Bind off all stitches in pattern.

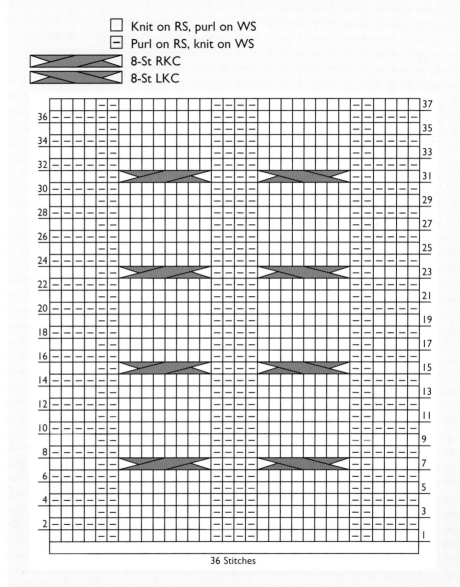

Knit on RS, purl on WS

Purl on RS, knit on WS

8-St RKC

8-St LKC

36 Stitches

BAMBOO CABLE

If you want to add some interest to a basic cable, vary the number of rows between the cable crossings. The result looks like bamboo.

BASIC PATTERN
Multiple of 4 stitches with 4 edge stitches (optional)

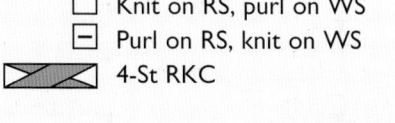

- ☐ Knit on RS, purl on WS
- ⊟ Purl on RS, knit on WS
- ▨ 4-St RKC

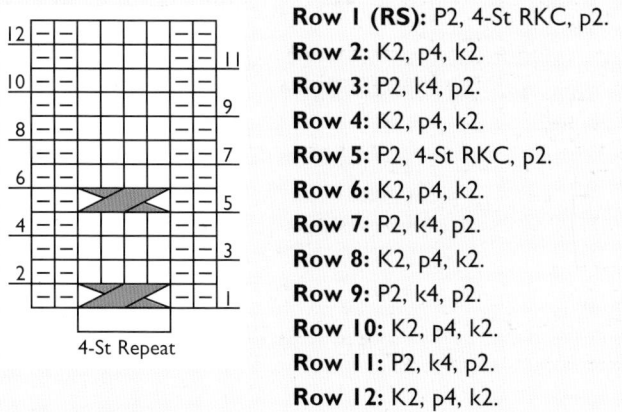

4-St Repeat

Row 1 (RS): P2, 4-St RKC, p2.
Row 2: K2, p4, k2.
Row 3: P2, k4, p2.
Row 4: K2, p4, k2.
Row 5: P2, 4-St RKC, p2.
Row 6: K2, p4, k2.
Row 7: P2, k4, p2.
Row 8: K2, p4, k2.
Row 9: P2, k4, p2.
Row 10: K2, p4, k2.
Row 11: P2, k4, p2.
Row 12: K2, p4, k2.
Repeat rows 1 – 12.

BAMBOO CABLE – MAKE A SWATCH

Cast on 32 stitches.

Row 1 (RS): [K4, p3] 4 times, k4.

Row 2: K7, p4, [k3, p4] twice, k7.

Row 3: K4, p3, 4-St RKC, p3, k4, p3, 4-St RKC, p3, k4.

Row 4: K7, p4, [k3, p4] twice, k7.

Row 5: [K4, p3] 4 times, k4.

Row 6: K7, p4, [k3, p4] twice, k7.

Row 7: K4, p3, 4-St RKC, p3, k4, p3, 4-St RKC, p3, k4.

Row 8: K7, p4, [k3, p4] twice, k7.

Row 9: [K4, p3] twice, 4-St RKC, [p3, k4] twice.

Row 10: K7, p4, [k3, p4] twice, k7.

Row 11: [K4, p3] 4 times, k4.

Row 12: K7, p4, [k3, p4] twice, k7.

Row 13: [K4, p3] twice, 4-St RKC, [p3, k4] twice.

Row 14: K7, p4, [k3, p4] twice, k7.

Rows 15 – 26: Repeat rows 3 – 14.

Rows 27 – 32: Repeat rows 3 – 8.

Row 33: Repeat row 1.

Bind off all stitches in patterns.

☐ Knit on RS, purl on WS

⊟ Purl on RS, knit on WS

▧ 4-St RKC

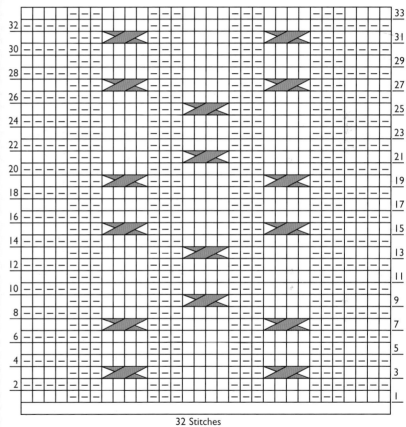

32 Stitches

SIMPLE SERPENTINE CABLE

By pairing right and left crosses above each other in a column, you create a serpentine cable. This is a fun and lively cable that is easy to knit.

BASIC PATTERN
Multiple of 6 stitches with 4 edge stitches *(optional)*

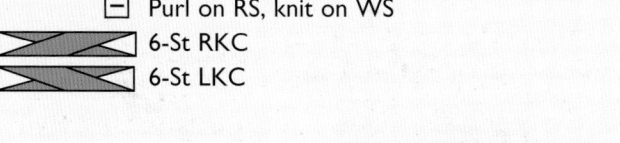

☐ Knit on RS, purl on WS
⊟ Purl on RS, knit on WS
▨ 6-St RKC
▨ 6-St LKC

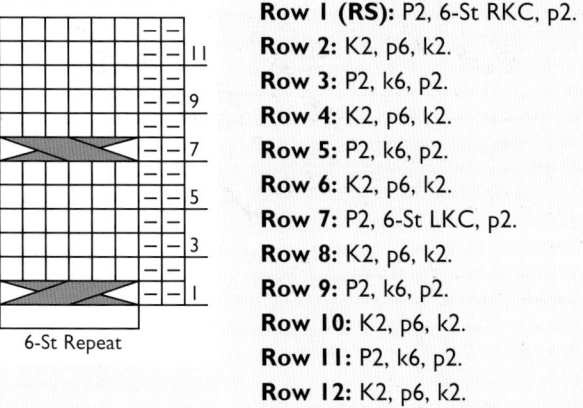

6-St Repeat

Row 1 (RS): P2, 6-St RKC, p2.
Row 2: K2, p6, k2.
Row 3: P2, k6, p2.
Row 4: K2, p6, k2.
Row 5: P2, k6, p2.
Row 6: K2, p6, k2.
Row 7: P2, 6-St LKC, p2.
Row 8: K2, p6, k2.
Row 9: P2, k6, p2.
Row 10: K2, p6, k2.
Row 11: P2, k6, p2.
Row 12: K2, p6, k2.
Repeat rows 1 – 12.

SIMPLE SERPENTINE CABLE – MAKE A SWATCH

Cast on 36 stitches.

Row 1 (RS): K1, p1, k1, p3 [k6, p3] 3 times, k1, p1, k1.

Row 2: K1, p1, k4, [p6, k3] 3 times, k1, p1, k1.

Row 3: K1, p1, k1, p3, 6-St RKC, p3, 6-St LKC, p3, 6-St RKC, p3, k1, p1, k1.

Row 4: K1, p1, k4, [p6, k3] 3 times, k1, p1, k1.

Row 5: K1, p1, k1, p3, [k6, p3] 3 times, k1, p1, k1.

Row 6: K1, p1, k4, [p6, k3] 3 times, k1, p1, k1.

Row 7: K1, p1, k1, p3, [k6, p3] 3 times, k1, p1, k1.

Row 8: K1, p1, k4, [p6, k3] 3 times, k1, p1, k1.

Row 9: K1, p1, k1, p3, 6-St LKC, p3, 6-St RKC, p3, 6-St LKC, p3, k1, p1, k1.

Row 10: K1, p1, k4, [p6, k3] 3 times, k1, p1, k1.

Row 11: K1, p1, k1, p3, [k6, p3] 3 times, k1, p1, k1.

Row 12: K1, p1, k4, [p6, k3] 3 times, k1, p1, k1.

Rows 13 – 24: Repeat rows 1 – 12.

Rows 25 – 29: Repeat rows 1 – 5.

Bind off all stitches in pattern.

Knit on RS, purl on WS

Purl on RS, knit on WS

6-St RKC

6-St LKC

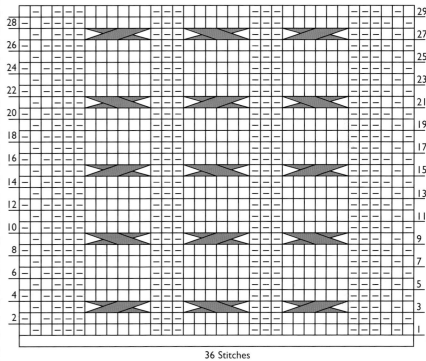

36 Stitches

27

SQUIGGLES AND BUMPS CABLE

This fun cable introduces two new techniques: Bobbles and purl cross cables. Bobbles (page 19) are raised balls of stiches, created by increasing several times in a single stitch and then knitting back and forth on the newly created stitches. Purl cross cables (pages 14 and 15) use knit and purl stitches together and are very effective in creating diagonal lines.

BASIC PATTERN
Multiple of 6 stitches with four edge stitches *(optional)*

☐	Knit on RS, purl on WS
⊟	Purl on RS, knit on WS
⊡	MB
⧄	3-St RPC
⧅	3-St LPC

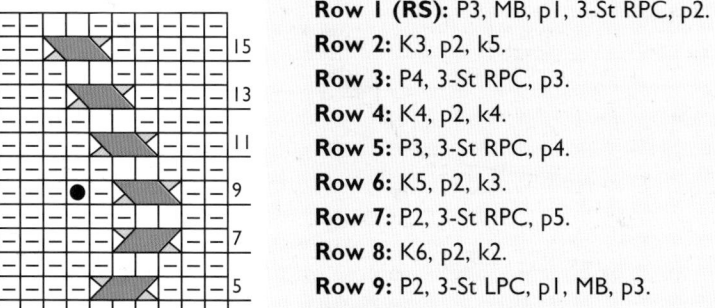

6-St Repeat

Row 1 (RS): P3, MB, p1, 3-St RPC, p2.
Row 2: K3, p2, k5.
Row 3: P4, 3-St RPC, p3.
Row 4: K4, p2, k4.
Row 5: P3, 3-St RPC, p4.
Row 6: K5, p2, k3.
Row 7: P2, 3-St RPC, p5.
Row 8: K6, p2, k2.
Row 9: P2, 3-St LPC, p1, MB, p3.
Row 10: K5, p2, k3.
Row 11: P3, 3-St LPC, p4.
Row 12: K4, p2, k4.
Row 13: P4, 3-St LPC, p3.
Row 14: K3, p2, k5.
Row 15: P5, 3-St LPC, p2.
Row 16: K2, p2, k6.
Repeat rows 1 – 16.

SQUIGGLES AND BUMPS CABLE –
MAKE A SWATCH

Cast on 44 stitches.

Row 1 (RS): K5, *p6, k2, p2, k2*; repeat from * to * until last 3 sts, k3.

Row 2: K3, *p2, k2, p2, k6*; repeat from * to * until last 5 sts, p2, k3.

Row 3: K5, *p6, k2, p2, k2*; repeat from * to * until last 3 sts, k3.

Row 4: K3, *p2, k2, p2, k6*; repeat from * to * until last 5 sts, p2, k3.

Row 5: K5, *p3, MB, p1, 3-St RPC, p2, k2*; repeat from * to * until last 3 sts, k3.

Row 6: K3, *p2, k3, p2, k5*; repeat from * to * until last 5 sts, p2, k3.

Row 7: K5, *p4, 3-St RPC, p3, k2*; repeat from * to * until last 3 sts, k3.

Row 8: K3, *p2, k4, p2, k4*; repeat from * to * until last 5 sts, p2, k3.

Row 9: K5, *p3, 3-St RPC, p4, k2*; repeat from * to * until last 3 sts, k3.

Row 10: K3, *p2, k5, p2, k3*; repeat from * to * until last 5 sts, p2, k3.

Row 11: K5, *p2, 3-St RPC, p5, k2*; repeat from * to * until last 3 sts, k3.

Row 12: K3, * p2, k6, p2, k2*; repeat from * to * until last 5 sts, p2, k3.

Row 13: K5, * p2, 3-St LPC, p1, MB, p3, k2*; repeat from * to * until last 3 sts, k3.

Row 14: K3, *p2, k5, p2, k3*; repeat from * to * until last 5 sts, p2, k3.

Row 15: K5, *p3, 3-St LPC, p4, k2*; repeat from * to * until last 3 sts, k3.

Row 16: K3, *p2, k4, p2, k4*; repeat from * to * until last 5 sts, p2, k3.

Row 17: K5, *p4, 3-St LPC, p3, k2*; repeat from * to * until last 3 sts, k3.

Row 18: K3, *p2, k3, p2, k5*; repeat from * to * until last 5 sts, p2, k3.

Row 19: K5, *p5, 3-St LPC, p2, k2*; repeat from * to * until last 3 sts, k3.

Row 20: K3, *p2, k2, p2, k6*; repeat from * to * until last 5 sts, p2, k3.

Rows 21 – 36: Repeat rows 5 – 20.

Rows 37 – 42: Repeat rows 5 – 10.

Row 43: K5, *p3, k2, p5, k2*; repeat from * to * until last 3 sts, k3.

Row 44: K3, *p2, k5, p2, k3*; repeat from * to * until last 5 sts, p2, k3.

Row 45: K5, *p3, k2, p5, k2*; repeat from * to * until last 3 sts, k3.

Bind off all stitches in pattern.

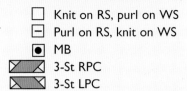

	Knit on RS, purl on WS
	Purl on RS, knit on WS
	MB
	3-St RPC
	3-St LPC

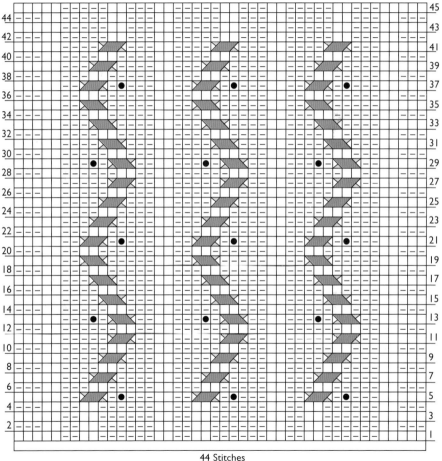

44 Stitches

LAPTOP COVER

My computer is my baby! It goes everywhere with me and I wanted a cover that would keep it padded but look great. By now, you've probably discovered that I love to combine yarn. In this design, hand painted wool is combined with an interesting multifiber boucle yarn.

FINISHED MEASUREMENTS
10" wide × 15" long (25.4 × 38.1 cm)

GAUGE
12 stitches and 17 rows = 4" (10 cm) in stockinette stitch
16 stitches and 20 rows = 4" (10 cm) in cable pattern

MATERIALS
Yarn A: Medium weight hand painted wool yarn,
approx 300 yd (274 m)
Yarn B: Medium weight multi fiber boucle yarn,
approx 135 yd (123 m)

THE YARN USED FOR THIS PROJECT
Yarn A: Dream in Color Handpainted Merino; 100% Australia Superwash
merino wool; 250 yd (229 m)/4 oz (113 g): 2 hanks, color
Strange Harvest #VM130
Yarn B: Berroco Trilogy; 32% wool, 28% cotton, 40% nylon;
80 yd (73 m)/1.75 oz (50 g): 2 hanks, color Edinburgh Rust #7609

NEEDLES AND NOTIONS
Size 11 (8 mm) knitting needles or size necessary to obtain correct gauge
Cable needle
Yarn needle for weaving in ends
Four buttons, 1" (2.5 cm) diameter with large holes and no shank

BEGINNING SECTION

First make the buttonholes on the front and establish the rib pattern in preparation for the main section. This section is made with two strands of the wool (Yarn A) held together.

BUTTONHOLE CHART

☐ Knit on RS, purl on WS

⊟ Purl on RS, knit on WS

☒ K2tog in knit stitches; P2tog in purl stitches

◙ Yarn Over (yo)

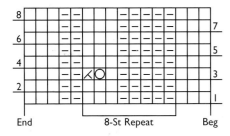

End   8-St Repeat   Beg

With 2 strands of Yarn A held together, cast on 40 stitches.

Row 1 (RS): K3, [p5, k3] 4 times, p2, k3.

Row 2: P3, k2, [p3, k5] 4 times, p3.

Row 3: K3, [p5, k1, yo, k2tog] 4 times, p2, k3.

Row 4: P3, k2, [p3, k5] 4 times, p3.

Row 5: K3, [p5, k3] 4 times, p2, k3.

Row 6: P3, k2, [p3, k5] 4 times, p3.

Row 7: K3, [p5, k3] 4 times, p2, k3.

Row 8: P3, k2, [p3, k5] 4 times, p3.

MAIN SECTION

The main section is knit with one strand each of the wool (Yarn A) and bouclé (Yarn B). The squiggles and bumps chart is repeated four times.

Cut 1 strand of Yarn A and replace it with 1 strand of Yarn B. Use 1 strand of Yarn A and Yarn B held together for the Main Section.

LAP TOP COVER CHART

☐ Knit on RS, purl on WS

⊟ Purl on RS, knit on WS

◉ MB

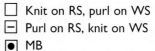 3-St RPC

3-St LPC

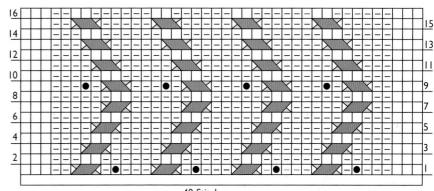

40 Stitches

IN THIS PATTERN, the stitches that precede the bobble are purl stitches, so be sure to move your yarn to the back before you start working on the bobble.

Row 1 (RS): K3, [p3, MB, p1, 3-St RPC] 4 times, p2, k3.
Row 2: P3, [k3, p2, k3] 4 times, k2, p3.
Row 3: K3, [p4, 3-St RPC, p1] 4 times, p2, k3.
Row 4: P3, k2, [k2, p2, k4] 4 times, p3.
Row 5: K3, [p3, 3-St RPC, p2] 4 times, p2, k3.
Row 6: P3, k2, [k3, p2, k3] 4 times, p3.
Row 7: K3, [p2, 3-St RPC, p3] 4 times, p2, k3.
Row 8: P3, k2, [k4, p2, k2] 4 times, p3.
Row 9: K3, [p2, 3-St LPC, p1, MB, p1] 4 times, p2, k3.
Row 10: P3, k2, [k3, p2, k3] 4 times, p3.
Row 11: K3, [p3, 3-St LPC, p2] 4 times, p2, k3.
Row 12: P3, k2, [k2, p2, k4] 4 times, p3.
Row 13: K3, [p4, 3-St LPC, p1] 4 times, p2, k3.
Row 14: P3, [k3, p2, k3] 4 times, k2, p3.
Row 15: K3, [p5, 3-St LPC] 4 times, p2, k3.
Row 16: P3, k2, [p2, k6] 4 times, p3.
Repeat rows 1 – 16 (4 times more).

ENDING SECTION

The ending section makes the back of the laptop case. The design continues with a plain rib that echoes the pattern on the front and also switches back to two strands of wool (Yarn A). *Note:* The back section is intentionally a bit shorter than the front section.

Cut the strand of Yarn B and replace with a second strand of Yarn A.
Row 1 (RS): K3, [p5, k3] 4 times, p2, k3.
Row 2: P3, k2, [p3, k5] 4 times, p3.
Repeat rows 1 – 2 until the length from the beginning is 30" (76.2 cm).
Bind off all stitches loosely keeping to rib pattern.

TO BIND OFF in pattern, work two stitches at a time in the usual way but knit or purl the stitches following the last row of the project pattern.

MAKE BOBBLE BUTTONS

The finishing touch is created by bobble buttons that match the bobbles on the cable. *Note:* when you cut the yarn be sure and leave the tails at least 8" (20.5cm) long to assemble the bobble and sew on the buttons.

With one strand of Yarn A and one strand of Yarn B held together, cast on 2 stitches.

K1, [k1, yo, k1, yo, k1] all into next stitch. You have 6 sts on the needle.

Working just the 5 stitches that have been made from the one stitch, turn, purl 5, turn, knit 5.

Turn, [p2tog] (3 times).

Turn, slip 1 st, k2tog, pass the slipped stitch over the stitch just worked. Cut yarn, leaving at least 8" (20.5 cm), and pull through last loop to fasten off.

Thread one strand of yarn from the tail on a yarn needle and work a running stitch around open edge of bobble. If desired, stuff a tiny ball of waste yarn into center of bobble, pull running stitch tight. Knot all four strands.

ASSEMBLING THE LAP TOP COVER

Fold the cover in half, wrong sides together, so the ribbed section is the back and the Cabled section is the front. Line up the short sides and invisibly stitch the long side seams.

ATTACH BUTTONS

The buttons are attached to the wrong side of the back (inside the case) opposite the buttonholes on the front.

Mark the location for the buttons.

Thread two strands of the yarn from bottom of bobble onto the tapestry needle.

Pass yarn from the inside to the outside of the Lap Top Cover. Repeat with the other two strands.

Working from outside, thread the yarn through holes on the button.

Tie a sturdy square knot and trim yarn ends to desired length.

FINISHING

Using a tapestry needle, weave in all ends. It is not necessary to block.

CLAW CABLE

I don't like calling this a claw cable—that sounds scary. It's soft and pretty so I much prefer paw or double. Whatever you call it, the cable can be worked in either an upward or downward direction.

BASIC PATTERN
Multiple of 12 stitches with 4 edge stitches *(optional)*

UPWARD CLAW
As shown on right side of swatch

- ☐ Knit on RS, purl on WS
- ⊟ Purl on RS, knit on WS
- 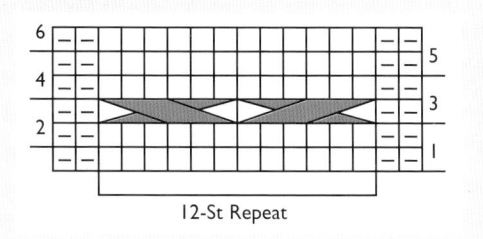 6-St RKC
- 6-St LKC

Row 1(RS): P2, k12, p2.
Row 2: K2, p12, k2.
Row 3: P2, 6-St RKC, 6-St LKC, p2.
Row 4: K2, p12, k2.
Rows 5: P2, k12, p2.
Row 6: K2, p12, k2.
Repeat rows 1 – 6.

12-St Repeat

DOWNWARD CLAW
As shown on left side of swatch

- ☐ Knit on RS, purl on WS
- ⊟ Purl on RS, knit on WS
- 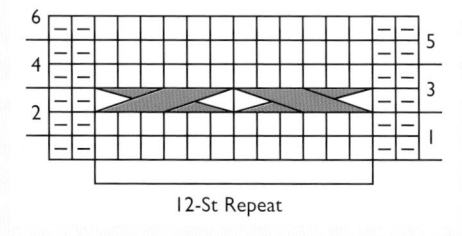 6-St RKC
- 6-St LKC

Row 1(RS): P2, k12, p2.
Row 2: K2, p12, k2.
Row 3: P2, 6-St LKC, 6 St RKC, p2.
Row 4: K2, p12, k2.
Rows 5: P2, k12, p2.
Row 6: K2, p12, k2.
Repeat rows 1 – 6.

12-St Repeat

CLAW CABLE – MAKE A SWATCH

Cast on 44 stitches.

Row 1 (RS): K1, p1, k1, p4, k12, p6, k12, p4, k1, p1, k1.

Row 2: K1, p1, k5, p12, k6, p12, k5, p1, k1.

Row 3: K1, p1, k1, p4, k12, p6, k12, p4, k1, p1, k1.

Row 4: K1, p1, k5, p12, k6, p12, k5, p1, k1.

Row 5: K1, p1, k1, p4, k12, p6, k12, p4, k1, p1, k1.

Row 6: K1, p1, k5, p12, k6, p12, k5, p1, k1.

Row 7: K1, p1, k1, p4, 6-St RKC, 6-St LKC, p6, 6-St LKC, 6-St RKC, p4, k1, p1, k1.

Rows 8 – 37: Repeat rows 2 – 7 (5 more times).

Row 38: K1, p1, k5, p12, k6, p12, k5, p1, k1.

Row 39: K1, p1, k1, p4, k12, p6, k12, p4, k1, p1, k1.

Row 40: K1, p1, k5, p12, k6, p12, k5, p1, k1.

Row 41: K1, p1, k1, p4, k12, p6, k12, p4, k1, p1, k1.

Row 42: K1, p1, k5, p12, k6, p12, k5, p1, k1.

Bind off all stitches in pattern.

□ Knit on RS, purl on WS
⊟ Purl on RS, knit on WS
6-St RKC
6-St LKC

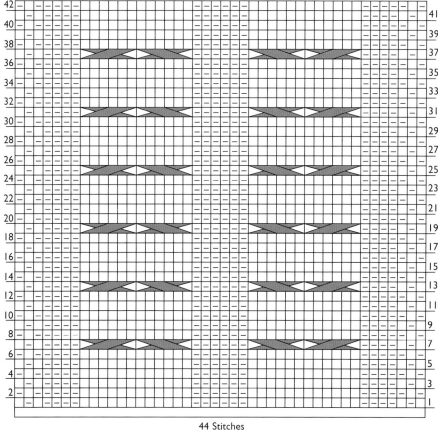

44 Stitches

PLAITED CABLE

This cable looks complicated but, in fact, it's easy to work. An 8-stitch cable is alternated from side to side within a 12-stitch band. The appearance of the cable varies depending on which direction the starting cable is worked.

BASIC PATTERN
Multiple of 12 stitches with 4 edge stitches (optional)

OUTWARD PLAIT

As Shown On Left Side Of Swatch

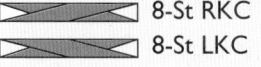

☐ Knit on RS, purl on WS
⊟ Purl on RS, knit on WS
▱ 8-St RKC
▱ 8-St LKC

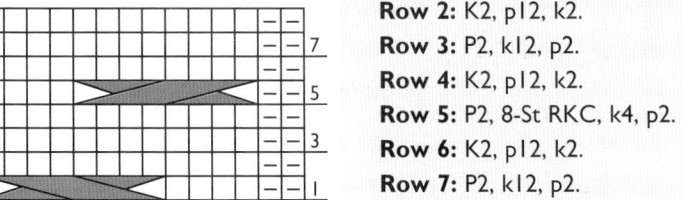

12-St Repeat

Row 1 (RS): P2, k4, 8-St LKC, p2.
Row 2: K2, p12, k2.
Row 3: P2, k12, p2.
Row 4: K2, p12, k2.
Row 5: P2, 8-St RKC, k4, p2.
Row 6: K2, p12, k2.
Row 7: P2, k12, p2.
Row 8: K2, p12, k2.
Repeat rows 1 – 8.

INWARD PLAIT

As Shown On Right Side Of Swatch

☐ Knit on RS, purl on WS
⊟ Purl on RS, knit on WS
▱ 8-St RKC
▱ 8-St LKC

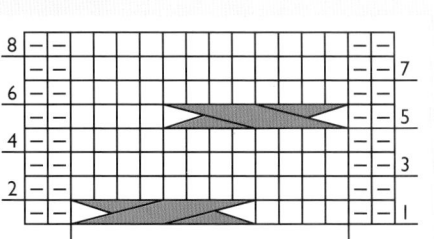

12-St Repeat

Row 1 (RS): P2, k4, 8-St RKC, p2.
Row 2: K2, p12, k2.
Row 3: P2, k12, p2.
Row 4: K2, p12, k2.
Row 5: P2, 8-St LKC, k4, p2.
Row 6: K2, p12, k2.
Row 7: P2, k12, p2.
Row 8: K2, p12, k2.
Repeat rows 1 – 8.

PLAITED CABLE – MAKE A SWATCH

Cast on 42 stitches.

Row 1 (RS): K1, p1, k1, p3, k12, p6, k12, p3, k1, p1, k1.

Row 2: K1, p1, k4, p12, k6, p12, k4, p1, k1.

Row 3: K1, p1, k1, p3, k4, 8-St RKC, p6, k4, 8-St LKC, p3, k1, p1, k1.

Row 4: K1, p1, k4, p12, k6, p12, k4, p1, k1.

Row 5: K1, p1, k1, p3, k12, p6, k12, p3, k1, p1, k1.

Row 6: K1, p1, k4, p12, k6, p12, k4, p1, k1.

Row 7: K1, p1, k1, p3, 8-St LKC, k4, p6, 8-St RKC, k4, p3, k1, p1, k1.

Row 8: K1, p1, k4, p12, k6, p12, k4, p1, k1.

Rows 9 – 40: Repeat rows 1 – 8 (4 more times).

Row 41: K1, p1, k, p3, k12, p6, k12, p3, k1, p1, k1.

Bind off all stitches in pattern.

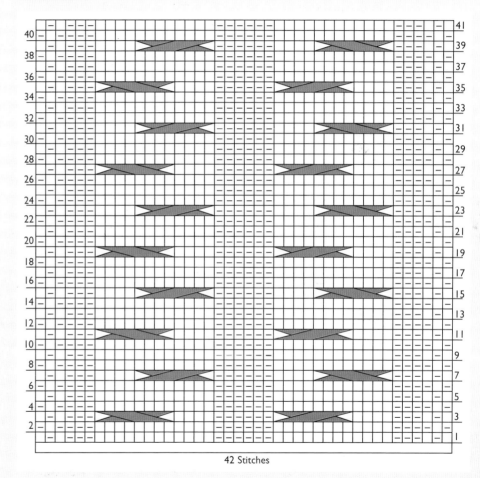

Knit on RS, purl on WS

Purl on RS, knit on WS

8-St RKC

8-St LKC

42 Stitches

HUGS AND KISSES CABLE

This design is interesting to work but not difficult.

One complete repeat of the pattern looks like a stack

of hugs (Os) and kisses (Xs).

BASIC PATTERN

Multiple of 8 stitches with 4 edge stitches *(optional)*

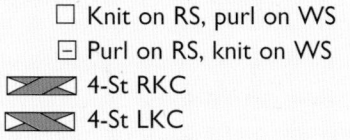

- ☐ Knit on RS, purl on WS
- ⊟ Purl on RS, knit on WS
- 4-St RKC
- 4-St LKC

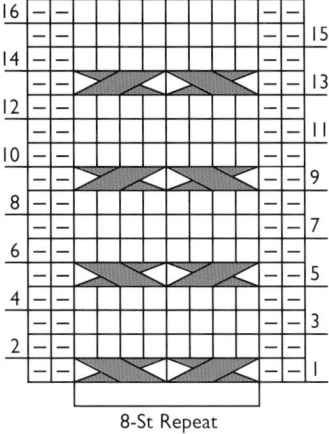

8-St Repeat

Row 1 (RS): P2, 4-St RKC, 4-St LKC, p2.
Row 2: K2, p8, k2.
Row 3: P2, k8, p2.
Row 4: K2, p8, k2.
Row 5: P2, 4-St RKC, 4-St LKC, p2.
Row 6: K2, p8, k2.
Row 7: P2, k8, p2.
Row 8: K2, p8, k2.
Row 9: P2, 4-St LKC, 4-St RKC, p2.
Row 10: K2, p8, k2.
Row 11: P2, k8, p2.
Row 12: K2, p8, k2.
Row 13: P2, 4-St LKC, 4-St RKC, p2.
Row 14: K2, p8, k2.
Row 15: P2, k8, p2.
Row 16: K2, p8, k2.
Repeat rows 1 – 16.

HUGS AND KISSES CABLE –
MAKE A SWATCH

Cast on 36 stitches.

Row 1 (RS): P1, k1, p1, k1, p4, [k8, p4] twice , k1, p1, k1, p1.

Row 2: K1, p1, k1, p1, k4, [p8, k4] (twice), p1, k1, p1, k1.

Row 3: P1, k1, p1, k1, p4, [4-St RKC, 4-St LKC, p4] twice, k1, p1, k1, p1.

Row 4: K1, p1, k1, p1, k4, [p8, k4] twice, p1, k1, p1, k1.

Row 5: P1, k1, p1, k1, p4, [k8, p4] twice, k1, p1, k1, p1.

Row 6: K1, p1, k1, p1, k4, [p8, k4] twice, p1, k1, p1, k1.

Row 7: P1, k1, p1, k1, p4, [4-St RKC, 4-St LKC, p4] twice, k1, p1, k1, p1.

Row 8: K1, p1, k1, p1, k4, [p8, k4] twice, p1, k1, p1, k1.

Row 9: P1, k1, p1, k1, p4, [k8, p4] twice, k1, p1, k1, p1.

Row 10: K1, p1, k1, p1, k4, [p8, k4] twice, p1, k1, p1, k1.

Row 11: P1, k1, p1, k1, p4, [4-St LKC, 4-St RKC, p4] twice, k1, p1, k1, p1.

Row 12: K1, p1, k1, p1, k4, [p8, k4] twice, p1, k1, p1, k1.

Row 13: P1, k1, p1, k1, p4, [k8, p4] twice, k1, p1, k1, p1.

Row 14: K1, p1, k1, p1, k4, [p8, k4] twice, p1, k1, p1, k1.

Row 15: P1, k1, p1, k1, p4, [4-St LKC, 4-St RKC, p4] twice, k1, p1, k1, p1.

Row 16: K1, p1, k1, p1, k4, [p8, k4] twice, p1, k1, p1, k1.

Rows 17 – 32: Repeat rows 1 – 16.

Bind off all stitches in pattern.

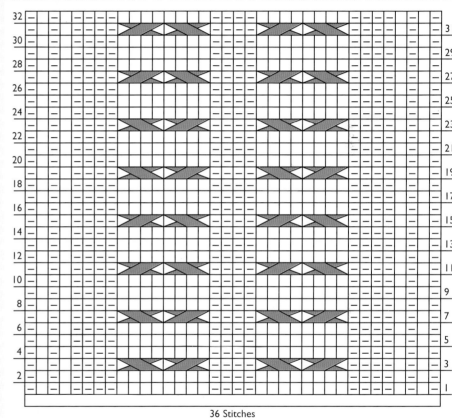

□ Knit on RS, purl on WS
⊟ Purl on RS, knit on WS
4-St RKC
4-St LKC

36 Stitches

KISS THE BABY SWEATER

Create a perfect baby sweater with the hugs and kisses cable.
The entire sweater is created from rectangles and squares
with just a bit of shaping for the front neck.

FINISHED MEASUREMENTS
Chest 20" (51 cm)
Length 10" (25 cm)

GAUGE
19 stitches and 32 rows = 4" (10 cm) in garter stitch

MATERIALS
Medium weight yarn, approx 300 yd (274 m)

THE YARN USED FOR THIS PROJECT
Rowan Soft Baby; 50% wool, 30% polyamide, 20% cotton,
    164 yd (150 m)/1.75 oz (50 g): 2 balls, color Princess #003

NEEDLES AND NOTIONS
Size 7 (4.5 mm) knitting needles or size necessary to obtain correct gauge
Cable needle
Yarn needle for weaving in ends
Button, ½" (13 mm) diameter

BACK
(Square shape)
You will begin and end with plain garter stitch (knit every row). In the main section, the cable is knit in the center.

BEGINNING SECTION
Cast on 48 stitches.
Knit every row until piece measures 3" (7.6 cm).

MAIN SECTION
Now you'll continue in garter stitch but insert the Hugs and Kisses Cable in the center of the back.

The first thing you'll need to do is add a few extra stitches as follows (this next row that you knit will become the right side).
Right Side: K22, inc in next 4 stitches, knit to end of row—52 sts.
Wrong Side: K22, p8, k22.

Keeping 22 stitches on either side in garter stitch, work the center 8 stitches in the Hugs and Kisses Cable. Using the cable chart on page 38, work as follows (note that you will begin with row 5 of the chart).
Row 1(RS): K22, (working row 5 of chart) 4-St RKC, 4-St LKC, k22.
Row 2: K22, p8, k22.
Row 3: Knit all stitches.
Row 4: K22, p8, k22.
Row 5: K22, (working row 9 of chart) 4-St LKC, 4-St RKC, k22.
Rows 6 – 8: Repeat rows 2 – 4.
Row 9: Repeat row 5 (working row 13 of chart).
Rows 10 – 12: Repeat rows 2 – 4.
Row 13: K22, (working row 1 of chart) 4-St RKC, 4-St LKC, k22.
Rows 14 – 16: Repeat rows 2 – 4.
Repeat rows 1 – 16 one more time.
Repeat rows 1 – 4.

At this point you'll work a special cable to eliminate the 4 stitches that were added at the beginning of the cable.

Right Side: K22, slip next 2 stitches to cable needle and hold in front, k2tog from left needle, k2tog from cable needle, slip next 2 stitches to cable needle and hold in back, k2tog from left needle, k2tog from cable needle, k22—48 sts.

ENDING SECTION
Switch back to working all stitches in garter stitch. Knit all rows until piece measures 10" (25.4 cm) from beginning. Bind off all stitches loosely.

RIGHT FRONT
(Rectangle shape with a bit of shaping for neck)
The fronts are similar to the back. However, instead of placing the cable in the center of the back, the cable is placed at one side of the rectangle. The cable motif is also longer, beginning after just a few rows of knitting.

BEGINNING SECTION
Cast on 24 stitches.
Knit in garter stitch for 4 rows.

MAIN SECTION
Just as you did on the back you will add 4 stitches to prepare to work the cable.
Right Side: K4, inc in next 4 stitches, k16—28 sts.
Wrong Side: K16, p8, k4.

Keeping 4 stitches on right edge (center front of sweater) and 16 stitches on left edge (side of sweater) in garter stitch, work 8 stitches in cable pattern by using cable chart beginning with row 1 as follows:

Row 1: K4, 4-St RKC, 4-St LKC, k16.
Row 2: K16, p8, k4.
Row 3: Knit all stitches.
Row 4: K16, p8, k4.
Rows 5 – 8: Repeat rows 1 – 4.
Row 9: K4, 4-St LKC, 4-St RKC, k16.
Rows 10 – 12: Repeat rows 2 – 4.
Rows 13 – 16: Repeat rows 9 – 12.
Repeat rows 1 – 16 (2 more times.)
Repeat rows 1 – 12 of chart (row 12 will be a wrong side row).

Eliminate 4 extra cable stitches.
RS: K4, slip next 2 stitches to cable needle and hold in front, k2tog from left needle, k2tog from cable needle, slip next 2 stitches to cable needle and hold in back, k2tog from left needle, k2tog from cable needle, k16—24 sts.

ENDING SECTION

Switch back to working all stitches in garter stitch. You will also work a buttonhole and shape the neck.
Knit 3 rows (the third row will be a wrong side row).
Make buttonhole as follows:
RS: K2, yo, k2tog, knit to end of row—24 sts.
Continue working all stitches in garter stitch until front measures 9" (23 cm) and you've just finished wrong side row.

WORK NECK SHAPING

RS: Bind off 6 sts, k to end of row—18 sts.
WS: Knit across.
RS: K1, k2tog, k to end of row—17 sts.
WS: Knit across.
RS: K1, k2tog, k to end of row—16 sts.
WS: Knit across.
RS: K1, k2tog, k to end of row—15 sts.
WS: Knit across.

Continue knitting until piece measures 10" (25 cm). Bind off all stitches loosely. Note: depending on your tension you may reach 10" (25 cm) as soon as you finish the decreases in which case you will bind off immediately.

LEFT FRONT

(Mirror image of the right front)

BEGINNING SECTION

Cast on 24 stitches.
Knit in garter stitch for 4 rows.

MAIN SECTION

RS: K16, k1f&b in next 4 stitches, k4—28 sts.
WS: K4, p8, 16.

Keeping 16 stitches on right edge (side of sweater) and 4 stitches on left edge (center front of sweater) in garter stitch, work 8 stitches in cable pattern by using Stitch Chart beginning with row 1 as follows:

Row 1: K16, 4-St RKC, 4-St LKC, k4.
Row 2: K4, p8, k16.
Row 3: Knit all stitches.
Row 4: K4. p8. k16.
Rows 5 – 8: Repeat rows 1 – 4.
Row 9: K16, 4-St LKC, 4-St RKC, k4.
Rows 10 – 12: Repeat rows 2 – 4.
Rows 13 – 16: Repeat rows 9 – 12.
Repeat rows 1 – 16 (2 more times).
Repeat rows 1 – 12 of chart (row 12 will be a wrong side row).

Eliminate 4 extra cable stitches.
RS: K16, slip next 2 stitches to cable needle and hold in front, k2tog from left needle, k2tog from cable needle, slip next 2 stitches to cable needle and hold in back, k2tog from left needle, k2tog from cable needle, k4—24 sts.

ENDING SECTION

Switch back to working all stitches in garter stitch until front measures
9" (23 cm) and you've just finished right side row.

WORK NECK SHAPING

WS: Bind off 6 sts, k to end of row—18 sts.
RS: Knit across.
WS: K1, k2tog, k to end of row—17 sts.
RS: Knit across.
WS: K1, k2tog, k to end of row—16 sts.
RS: Knit across.
WS: K1, k2tog, k to end of row—15 sts.
RS: Knit across.

Continue knitting until piece measures 10" (25 cm). Bind off all stitches loosely.

SLEEVES

(Make 2 rectangles with a cable on the side edge)
By now you are an expert at inserting the cable into your knitting. Note that the sleeves are knit from side seam to side seam.

BEGINNING SECTION

Cast on 28 stitches:
Knit in garter stitch for 6 rows.

MAIN SECTION

Increase Stitches
RS: K4, inc in next 4 sts, k20—32 sts.
WS: K20, p8, k4.

Keeping 4 stitches on right edge (cuff) and 20 stitches on left edge in garter stitch, work 8 stitches in cable pattern by using cable chart beginning with row 1.

Row 1: K4, 4-St RKC, 4-St LKC, k20.
Row 2: K20, p8, k4.
Row 3: Knit all stitches.
Row 4: K20, p8, k4.
Rows 5 – 8: Repeat rows 1 – 4.
Row 9: K4, 4-St LKC, 4-St RKC, k20.
Rows 10 – 12: Repeat rows 2 – 4.
Rows 13 – 16: Repeat rows 9 – 12.
Repeat rows 1 – 16 (2 more times).

Repeat rows 1 – 4 of chart (row 4 will be a wrong side row).
Eliminate 4 extra cable stitches.
RS: K4, [k2tog] 4 times, k20—28 sts.

ENDING SECTION

Knit 6 rows.
Bind off all stitches loosely.

FINISHING

Very lightly steam block the pieces using a steam iron set on wool setting. Don't allow the iron to touch the knitting.

SEW SEAMS

The best method to seam the sweater is invisible seaming (mattress stitch) which is worked from the right side. Lightly steam the seams as you work, finger pressing them to reduce the seam bulk.

• Using knitting yarn, sew shoulder seams.

• To attach the sleeves, find the center of sleeve along top edge
(the opposite edge from the cable). Lay the sweater flat, match
center of sleeve to shoulder seam. Seam the sleeve to the body.

• Sew the side and sleeve seams.

MAKE COLLAR

Working from the right side, pick up and knit 15 stitches from the right front neck edge, 18 stitches from the back neck edge, and 15 stitches from the left front neck edge—48 sts.
Row 1 (WS): Purl across.
Row 2: Knit across.
Rows 3 – 4: Repeat rows 1 – 2.
Bind off from wrong side using knit stitch.

Using a tapestry needle, weave in all ends. Attach button to left front in line with buttonhole on right front. Put the sweater on your favorite baby and give the baby a hug and kiss.

HONEYCOMB CABLE

This design is worked in a multiple of 8 stitches. It's a good filler and very easy to learn. After a few repeats, you'll be able to memorize the pattern.

BASIC PATTERN
Multiple of 8 stitches with 4 edge stitches *(optional)*

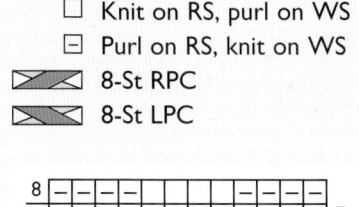

☐ Knit on RS, purl on WS
⊟ Purl on RS, knit on WS
8-St RPC
8-St LPC

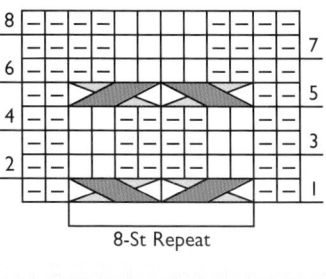

8-St Repeat

Row 1 (RS): P2, 4-St RPC, 4-St LPC, p2.
Row 2: K2, p2, k4, p2, k2.
Row 3: P2, k2, p4, k2, p2.
Row 4: K2, p2, k4, p2, k2.
Row 5: P2, 4-st LPC, 4-St RPC, p 2.
Row 6: K4, p4, k4.
Row 7: P4, k4, p4.
Row 8: K4, p4, k4.
Repeat rows 1 – 8.

HONEYCOMB CABLE – MAKE A SWATCH

Cast on 40 stitches.

Row 1(RS): K6, [p4, k4] 4 times, k2.

Row 2: K4, p2, [k4, p4] 3 times, k4, p2, k4.

Row 3: K6, [p4, k4] 4 times, k2.

Row 4: K4, p2, [k4, p4] 3 times, k4, p2, k4.

Row 5: K4, [4-St LPC, 4-St RPC] 4 times, k4.

Row 6: K6, [p4, k4] 4 times, k2.

Row 7: K4, p2, [k4, p4] 3 times, k4, p2, k4.

Row 8: K6, [p4, k4] 4 times, k2.

Row 9: K4, [4-St RPC, 4-St LPC] 4 times, k4.

Row 10: K4, p2, [k4, p4] 3 times, k4, p2, k4.

Row 11: K6, [p4, k4] 4 times, k2.

Row 12: K4, p2, [k4, p4] 3 times, k4, p2, k4.

Rows 13 – 36: Repeat rows 5 – 12 (3 more times).

Rows 37: K6, [p4, k4] 4 times, k2.

Rows 38: K4, p2, [k4, p4] 3 times, k4, p2, k4.

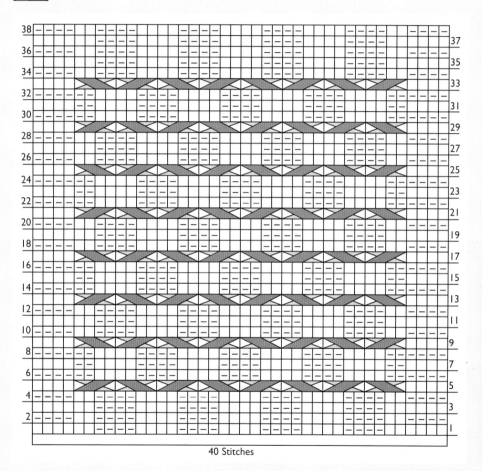

□	Knit on RS, purl on WS
⊟	Purl on RS, knit on WS
▨	4-St RPC
▨	4-St LPC

40 Stitches

| # EVENING BAG

Handbags with cable designs are very popular right now. This lovely evening bag is a simple yet elegant interpretation of that trend. A decrease is worked into the cable as it moves up the bag creating a dramatic tapered shape.

FINISHED MEASUREMENTS
12" wide at × 8½" tall (30.5 × 21.6 cm) (not including handle)

GAUGE
14 stitches and 20 rows = 4" (10 cm) in stockinette stitch
 with larger needle
22 stitches and 20 rows = 4" (10 cm) in cable pattern

MATERIALS
Medium weight multifiber yarn, approx 185 yd/170 m

THE YARN USED FOR THIS PROJECT
Plymouth Magnum; 42% rayon, 24% acrylic, 23% cotton, 9% nylon,
 2% polyester; 50 yd (46 m)/1.75 oz/50 g): 4 balls, color Blue #2110

NEEDLES AND NOTIONS
Size 9 (5.5 mm) needles or size necessary to obtain gauge
Size 10 (6 mm) needles
Cable needle
Yarn needle for weaving in ends
Sewing needle
Fabric for lining bag
Purse handle 6½" (16.5 cm) wide (the handle shown is available from Lacis)

EVENING BAG CHART

☐ Knit on RS, purl on WS

⊟ Purl on RS, knit on WS

☒ K2tog in knit stitiches;
   P2tog in purl stitches

☒ SSK

▨ 4-St RPC

▨ 4-St LPC

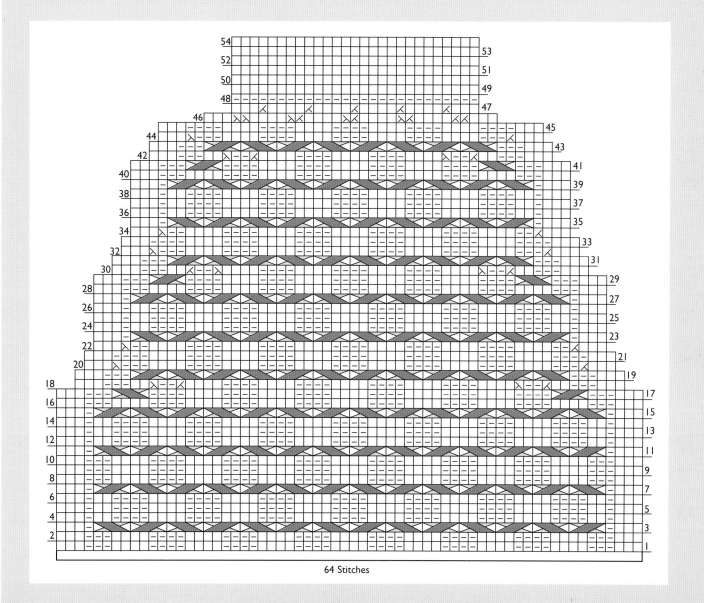

64 Stitches

FRONT AND BACK
(Make 2)

BEGINNING SECTION

To start, establish the honeycomb pattern
Using larger needles, cast on 64 stitches.

Row 1 (RS): K3, p3, k4, [p4, k4] 6 times, p3, k3.
Row 2: P3, k3, p4 [k4, p4] 6 times, k3, p3.
Row 3: K3, p1, [4-St RPC, 4-St LPC] 7 times, p1, k3.
Row 4: P3, k1, p2, k4, [p4, k4] 6 times, p2, k1, p3.
Row 5: K3, p1, k2, p4, [k4, p4] 6 times, k2, p1, k3.
Row 6: P3, k1, p2, k4, [p4, k4] 6 times, p2, k1, p3.
Row 7: K3, p1, [4-St LPC, 4-St RPC] 7 times, p1, k3.
Row 8: P3, k3, p4 [k4, p4] 6 times, k3, p3.
Rows 9-16: Repeat rows 1 – 8.

MAIN SECTION

Some special cables and decreases are worked along the side in order to taper the shape of the bag.

Row 17: K3, p3, 4-St RPC, p4 [k4, p4] 5 times, 4-St LPC, p3, k3.
Row 18: P3, k3, p2, ssk, k2, k2tog, p4, [k4, p4] 4 times, ssk, k2, k2tog, p2, k3, p3 – 60 sts.
Row 19: K3, p3, [4-St LPC, 4-St RPC] 6 times, p3, k3.
Row 20: P3, ssk, k3, p4, [k4, p4] 5 times, k3, k2tog, p3 – 58 sts.
Row 21: K3, p4, [k4, p4] 6 times, k3.
Row 22: P3, ssk, k2, p4, [k4, p4] 5 times, k2, k2tog, p3 – 56 sts.
Row 23: K3, p1, [4-St RPC, 4-St LPC] 6 times, p1, k3.
Row 24: P3, k1, p2, k4 [p4, k4] 5 times, p2, k1, p3.
Row 25: K3, p1, k2, p4, [k4, p4] 5 times, k2, p1, k3.
Row 26: P3, k1, p2, k4 [p4, k4] 5 times, p2, k1, p3.

Row 27: K3, p1, [4-St LPC, 4-St RPC] 6 times, p1, k3.
Row 28: P3, k3, p4, [k4, p4] 5 times, k3, p3.
Row 29: K3, p3, 4-St LPC, p4, [k4, p4] 4 times, 4-St RPC, p3, k3.
Row 30: P3, k3, p2, ssk, k2, k2tog, p4, [k4, p4] 3 times, ssk, k2, k2tog, p2, k3, p3 – 52 sts.
Row 31: K3, p3, [4-St LPC, 4-St LPC] 5 times, p3, k3
Row 32: P3, ssk, k3, p4, [k4, p4] 4 times, k3, k2tog, p3 – 50 sts.
Row 33: K3, p4, [k4, p4] 5 times, k3.
Row 34: P3, ssk, k2, p4, [k4, p4] 4 times, k2, k2tog, p3 – 48 sts.
Row 35: K3, p1, [4-St RPC, 4-St LPC] 5 times, p1, k3.
Row 36: P3, k1, p2, k4, [p4, k4] 4 times, p2, k1, p3.
Row 37: K3, p1, k2, p4, [k4, p4] 4 times, k2, p1, k3.
Row 38: P3, k1, p2, k4, [p4, k4] 4 times, p2, k1, p3.
Row 39: K3, p1, [4-St LPC, 4-St RPC] 5 times, p1, k3.
Row 40: P3, k3, p4, [k4. p4] 4 times, k3, p3.
Row 41: K3, p3, 4-St LPC, p4, [k4, p4] 3 times, 4-St RPC, p3, k3.
Row 42: P3, k3, p2, ssk, k2, k2tog, p4, [k4, p4] 2 times, ssk, k2, k2tog, p2, k3, p3 – 44 sts.
Row 43: K3, p3, [4-St LPC, 4-St RPC] 4 times, p3, k3.
Row 44: P3, ssk, k3, p4, [k4, p4] 3 times, k3, k2tog, p3 – 42 sts.
Row 45: K3, p4, [k4, p4] 4 times, k3.
Row 46: P3, ssk, ssk, p4, [ssk, k2tog, p4] 3 times, k2tog, k2tog, p3 – 32 sts.
Row 47: K3, p2tog, [k4, p2tog] 4 times, k3 – 27 sts.

ENDING SECTION

Now make a stockinette stitch flap that will be turned to the inside of the bag.

Row 48: Change to smaller needles and knit all sts to make a turning row.
49: Knit
50: Purl
Rows 51 – 54: Repeat rows 49-50 (two more times)
Bind off.

FINISHING

- Using the yarn needle, weave in all ends.

- Lightly steam block using a steam iron set on wool and never allowing the iron to get any closer than three inches to the bag. Pay particular attention to the tapered edge tugging gently to straighten out any unevenness.

- If desired, line bag with fabric. Cut fabric about 1" (2.5 cm) larger than bag sections on all sides. Turn edges under so that lining is about $\frac{1}{4}$" (6 mm) smaller than bag on all sides and pin into place on wrong side of bag. Stitch on all four sides using sewing thread.

- With right sides facing, pin sides and bottom of bag. Using sewing thread doubled, stitch bag together on sides and bottom leaving top 2½" (6.4 cm) open on both sides to accommodate handle. Use a backstitch and be sure to add a few extra stitches on the sides where the seam ends.

- Fold top to wrong side at turning ridge and stitch into place along bound off edge.

- Turn bag right side out. Steam very gently to smooth out the seams at the side and bottom.

- Unscrew end on horizontal bar of bag handle. Insert bar through bag casing and handle and re-attach screw.

TWISTED CHAIN CABLE

In this cable pattern, basic cables meander in and out of each other to create a fascinating design. The result looks like a beautiful chain.

BASIC PATTERN
Multiple of 16 stitches with 4 edge stitches *(optional)*

- ☐ Knit on RS, purl on WS
- ⊟ Purl on RS, knit on WS
- 4-St RPC
- 4-St LKC
- 4-St LPC

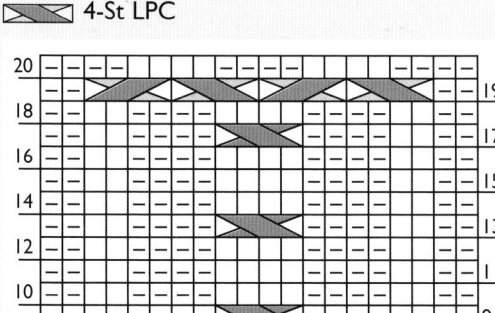

16-St Repeat

Row 1 (RS): P4, [4-St LKC, p4] twice.

Row 2: K4, [p4, k4] twice.

Row 3: P4, [k4, p4] twice.

Row 4: K4, [p4, k4] twice.

Row 5: P4, [4-St LKC, p4] twice.

Row 6: K4, [p4, k4] twice.

Row 7: P2, [4-St RPC, 4-St LPC] twice, p2.

Row 8: K2, p2, k4, p4, k4, p2, k2.

Row 9: P2, k2, p4, 4-St LKC, p4, k2, p2.

Row 10: K2, p2, k4, p4, k4, p2, k2.

Row 11: P2, k2, p4, k4, p4, k2, p2.

Row 12: K2, p2, k4, p4, k4, p2, k2.

Row 13: P2, k2, p4, 4-St LKC, p4, k2, p2.

Row 14: K2, p2, k4, p4, k4, p2, k2.

Row 15: P2, k2, p4, k4, p4, k2, p2.

Row 16: K2, p2, k4, p4, k4, p2, k2.

Row 17: P2, k2, p4, 4-St LKC, p4, k2, p2.

Row 18: K2, p2, k4, p4, k4, p2, k2.

Row 19: P2, [4-St LPC, 4-St RPC] twice, p2.

Row 20: K4, [p4, k4] twice.

Repeat rows 1 – 20.

TWISTED CHAIN CABLE – MAKE A SWATCH

Cast on 46 stitches.

Row 1 (RS): K3, [p4, k4] twice, p8, [k4, p4] twice, k3.

Row 2: K3, [k4, p4] twice, k8, [p4, k4] twice, k3.

Row 3: K3, [p4, 4-St LKC] twice, p8, [4-St LKC, p4] twice, k3.

Row 4: K3, [k4, p4] twice, k8, [p4, k4] twice, k3.

Row 5: K3, [p4, k4] twice, k8, [k4, p4]twice, k3.

Row 6: K3, [k4, p4] twice, k8, [p4, k4] twice, k3.

Row 7: K3, [p4, 4-St LKC] twice, p8,
[4-St LKC, p4] twice, k3.

Row 8: K3, [k4, p4] twice, k8, [p4, k4] twice, k3.

Row 9: K3, p2, [4-St RPC, 4-St LPC] twice, p4,
[4-St RPC, 4-St LPC] twice, p2, k3.

Row 10: K3, [k2, p2, k4, p4, k4, p2, k2] twice, k3.

Row 11: K3, [p2, k2, p4, 4-St LKC, p4, k2, p2] twice, k3.

Row 12: K3, [k2, p2, k4, p4, k4, p2, k2] twice, k3.

Row 13: K3, [p2, k2, p4, k4, p4, k2, p2] twice, k3.

Row 14: K3, [k2, p2, k4, p4, k4, p2, k2] twice, k3.

Row 15: K3, [p2, k2, p4, 4-St LKC, p4, k2, p2] twice, k3.

Row 16: K3, [k2, p2, k4, p4, k4, p2, k2] twice, k3.

Row 17: K3, [p2, k2, p4, k4, p4, k2, p2] twice, k3.

Row 18: K3, [k2, p2, k4, p4, k4, p2, k2] twice, k3.

Row 19: K3, [p2, k2, p4, 4-St LKC, p4, k2, p2] twice, k3.

Row 20: K3, [k2, p2, k4, p4, k4, p2, k2] twice, k3.

Row 21: K3, p2, [4-St LPC, 4-St RPC] twice, p4,
[4-St LPC, 4-St RPC] twice, p2, k3.

Rows 22 – 41: Repeat rows 2 – 21.

Rows 42 – 48: Repeat rows 2 – 8.

Bind off all stitches in pattern.

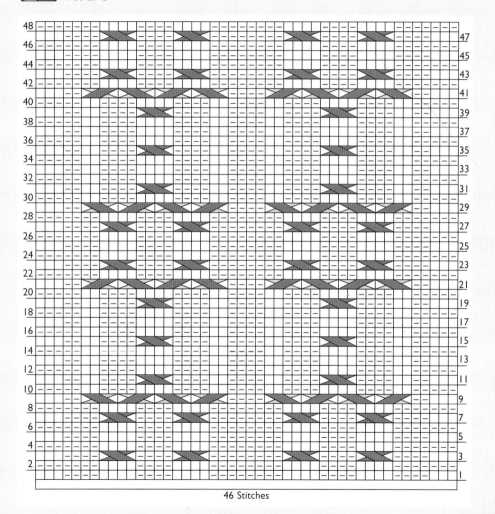

☐ Knit on RS, purl on WS
⊟ Purl on RS, knit on WS
▨ 4-St RPC
▨ 4-St LKC
▨ 4-St LPC

46 Stitches

| # HEMP MESSENGER BAG

Need to impress the 'in crowd'? Knit this messenger bag made from two strands of hemp held together. The flap is embellished with numerous cables while the rest of the bag is knit in plain reverse stockinette stitch with a single cable at each edge. The strap is made from a skinny, cabled band that is inserted into the body of the bag to form a gusset.

FINISHED MEASUREMENTS
Bag 12½" (31.8 cm) wide by 10" (25.4 cm) tall
Strap 44" (112 cm) long

GAUGE
15 stitches and 20 rows = 4" (10 cm) in reverse stockinette stitch
25 stitches and 22 rows = 4" (10 cm) in cable pattern

MATERIALS
Light weight hemp yarn, approx 710 yd (650 m)

THE YARN USED FOR THIS PROJECT
Lana Knits Hemp for Knitting allhemp6; 100% hemp; 165 yd (150 m)/3.5 oz (100 g): 5 hanks, color Charcoal #014

NEEDLES AND NOTIONS
Size 6 (4 mm) knitting needles or size necessary to obtain correct gauge
Cable needle
Yarn needle for weaving in ends
Fabric for lining bag, optional

TWIST CHAIN MESSENGER BAG CHART

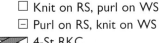

☐ Knit on RS, purl on WS
⊟ Purl on RS, knit on WS

 4-St RKC
4-St RPC
4-St LKC
4-St LPC

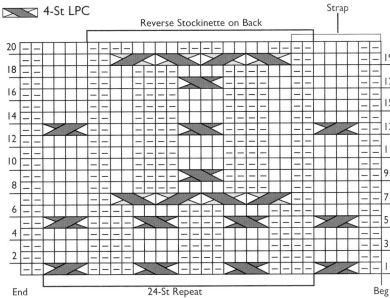

Strap

Reverse Stockinette on Back

End   24-St Repeat   Beg

FOR EASE IN working with a large number of stitches, use longer needles or a circular needle to work back and forth.

This pattern is knit throughout with two strands of yarn held together.

FLAP
BEGINNING SECTION
With 2 strands of yarn held together, cast on 80 stitches.
Foundation Row (WS): K2, * p4, k4 *; repeat from * to * last 6 stitches, p4, k2

MAIN SECTION
Next, work the main portion of the cabled flap using Messenger Bag Chart.
Row 1 (RS): P2, 4-St RKC, *[p4, 4-St LKC] twice, p4, 4-St RKC*;
repeat from * to * until last 2 stitches, p2.
Row 2: K2, *p4, k4*; repeat from * to * until last 6 stitches, p4, k2.
Row 3: P2, k4, *p4, k4*; from * to * until last 2 stitches, p2.
Row 4: K2, *p4, k4*; repeat from * to * until last 6 stitches, p4, k2.
Row 5: P2, 4-St RKC, *[p4, 4-St LKC] twice, p4, 4-St RKC*;
repeat from * to * until last 2 stitches, p2.
Row 6: K2, *p4, k4*; repeat from * to * until last 6 stitches, p4, k2.
Row 7: P2, k4, *p2, [4-St RPC, 4-St LPC] twice, p2, k4*;
repeat from * to * until last 2 stitches, p2.
Row 8: K2, *p4, k2, p2, k4, p4, k4, p2, k2*; from * to * until last 6 stitches, p4, k2.
Row 9: P2, k4, *p2, k2, p4, 4-St LKC, p4, k2, p2, k4*;
from * to * until last 2 stitches, p2.
Row 10: Repeat row 8.
Row 11: P2, k4, *p2, k2, p4, k4, p4, k2, p2, k4*;
from * to * until last 2 stitches, p2.
Rows 12: Repeat row 8.
Row 13: P2, 4-St RKC, *p2, k2, p4, 4-St LKC, p4, k2, p2, 4-St RKC *;
from * to * until last 2 stitches, p2.
Row 14: Repeat row 8.
Row 15: Repeat row 11.
Row 16: Repeat row 8.
(continued on next page)

(continued)

Row 17: Repeat row 9.
Row 18: Repeat row 8.
Row 19: P2, k4, *p2, [4-St LPC, 4-St RPC] twice, p2, k4*; repeat from * to * until last 2 stitches, p2.
Row 20: Repeat row 2.
Repeat rows 1 – 20 (once more).
Repeat rows 1 – 6. You have a total of 47 rows from beginning.

ENDING SECTION

This section will decrease a number of stitches to prepare for knitting the body of the bag.
Row 48: P2, k4, p4, *[k2tog] twice, p4*; repeat from * to * until last 6 sts, k4, p2—64 sts.
Row 49: K2, p4, k4, *p2, k4*; repeat from * to * until last 6 sts, k4, p2.
Row 50: P2, k4, p3, [p2tog] twice, *p2, [p2tog] twice* repeat from * to * until last 9 sts, p3, k4, p2 – 48 sts.
Row 51: K2, p4, knit to last 6 sts, p4, k2.
Row 52: P2, k4, purl to last 6 sts, k4, p2.
Row 53: K2, *p4, k2, p2, k4, p4, k2, k2*; repeat from * to * until last 6 stitches, p4, k2.

BODY OF BAG
MAIN SECTION

At this point, begin again with row 1 of the chart. You will keep repeating the 20 rows of the chart for the first and last cable as established but the center section will be worked in reverse stockinette stitch.
Row 1 (RS): P2, 4-St RKC, p to last 6 sts, 4-St RKC, p2.

Row 2: K2, p4, k to last 6 sts, p4, k2.
Row 3: P2, k4, p to last 6 sts, k4, p2.
Row 4: K2, p4, k to last 6 sts, p4, k2.
Row 5: P2, k4, p to last 6 sts, k4, p2.
Row 6: K2, p4, k to last 6 sts, p4, k2.
Row 7: P2, k4, p to last 6 sts, k4, p2.
Row 8: K2, p4, k to last 6 sts, p4, k2.
Row 9: P2, 4-St RKC, p to last 6 sts, 4-St RKC, p2.
Row 10: K2, p4, k to last 6 sts, p4, k2.
Row 11: P2, k4, p to last 6 sts, k4, p2.
Row 12: K2, p4, k to last 6 sts, p4, k2.
Row 13: P2, 4-St RKC, p to last 6 sts, 4-St RKC, p2.
Rows 14 – 20: Repeat rows 2 – 8.
Repeat rows 1 – 20 (4 more times).
Repeat rows 1 – 2 (total of 155 rows from the beginning).

ENDING SECTION

A few rows of plain garter stitch complete the body of the bag.
Knit 4 rows. Bind off all stitches loosely.

STRAP/GUSSET

The strap is easy to make, it's just the side cable from the body of the bag (8 stitches) knit by itself. The part of the strap that becomes the side of the bag is known as the gusset but it's all knit the same way in a single piece.

Knit a short section to get ready for the cable.
With 2 strands of yarn held together, cast on 8 sts.
Row 1 (RS): P2, k4, p2.
Row 2: K2, p4, k2.
Rows 3 – 6: Repeat rows 1 – 2 (2 more times).

MAIN SECTION

Row 1: P2, 4-St RKC, p2.
Row 2: K2, p4, k2.
Row 3: P2, k4, p2.
Row 4: K2, p4, k2.
Row 5: P2, 4-St RKC, p2.
Row 6: K2, p4, k2.
Row 7: P2, k4, p2.
Row 8: K2, p4, k2.
Row 9: P2, k4, p2.
Row 10: K2, p4, k2.
Row 11: P2, k4, p2.
Row 12: K2, p4, k2.
Row 13: P2, 4-St RKC, p2.
Rows 14 – 20: Repeat rows 6 – 12.
Repeat rows 1 – 20 (14 more times).

A total of 306 rows have been worked.
The strap/gusset above is about 64" (163 cm) long; 10" (25 cm on either side will become the bag gusset which will leave a strap about 44" (112 cm) long. If you want a shorter strap then don't repeat rows 1 – 20 as many times but be sure to omit a

full repeat so that the strap will finish at the correct point on the cables design.

Bind off all stitches.

ASSEMBLE BAG

• Fold the body of the bag so that the ending rows (the garter stitch section) match the beginning of the body section. Mark the center of the fold on both sides, this should be in the middle of a double cable section (where the cables have only three plain rows between crossings). Pin the strap to the body of the bag so that the center of the cast on edge matches the mark made on the bag. Pinning as you go, wrap the body of the bag around the bottom edge of the strap and then along the side; repeat for other side of strap. The strap will form a gusset and the cables from the strap and the bag will match.

• Working from the right side, invisibly seam the gusset (strap) to the bag. Beginning at the back, stitch the seam down to the fold, across the cast-on edge of the strap, and then back up to the front of the bag (the garter stitch section of the body).

• Repeat for other side. The only difference is that you will be working with the bound-off edge of the strap instead of the cast-on edge. Don't forget to line up the cables of the strap with the cables on the bag. Also, don't forget that knitting is a work of art, not of engineering. If the cables don't

match perfectly—don't worry, be happy. The bag is made from hemp. Get it?

FINISHING

• Using the tapestry needle, weave in all ends.

For bags knit from hemp only:

• Immerse the bag in warm water and allow it to soak for a few minutes. Wrap in a towel to remove excess moisture. Dry in a clothes dryer set on medium heat until just damp. Stuff with plastic bags to shape and allow it to dry completely. Once dry, steam flap with steam iron set on cotton setting. **Note: Do not follow this step unless the yarn you've used can be washed in this manner. If you're not certain then skip this step.**

• If desired, line body section and gusset with fabric. Cut fabric pieces about 1" (2.5 cm) wider than the body section and twice as long as folded length. Turn the raw edges under so that lining is about ¼" (6 mm) smaller than bag on all sides.

• Turn the bag inside out. Starting at the top of the bag (the garter stitch section), wrapping across the bottom and ending where the bag body meets the flap, pin the fabric into place on wrong side of bag. Stitch on all four sides using sewing thread.

• Line the strap/gusset in the same manner.

55

ENCLOSED CABLE

At first glance this cable seems complicated. However, it is just one basic cable enclosed within another and at both the bottom and top there is a plaited cable. You can do this!

BASIC PATTERN
Multiple of 20 stitches with 4 edge stitches *(optional)*

□ Knit on RS, purl on WS
⊟ Purl on RS, knit on WS
5-St RPC
5-St LPC
6-St RKC
6-St LKC

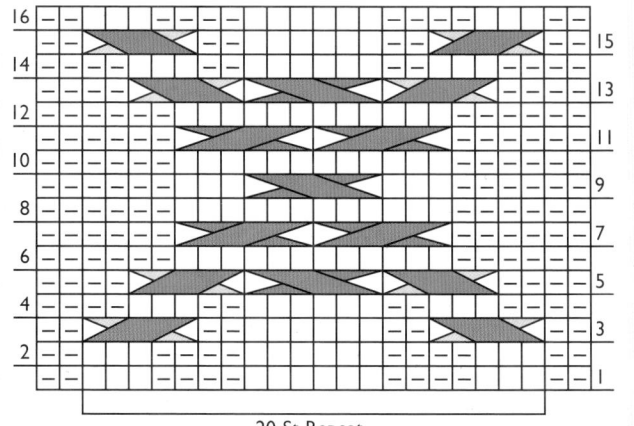

20-St Repeat

Row 1(RS): P2, k3, p4, k6, p4, k3, p2.

Row 2: K2, p3, k4, p6, k4, p3, k2.

Row 3: P2, 5-St LPC, p2, k6, p2, 5-St RPC, p2.

Row 4: K4, p3, k2, p6, k2, p3, k4.

Row 5: P4, 5-St LPC, 6-St LKC, 5-St RPC, p4.

Row 6: K6, p12, k6.

Row 7: P6, [6-St RKC] twice, p6.

Row 8: K6, p12, k6.

Row 9: P6, k3, 6-St LPC, k3, p6.

Row 10: K6, p12, k6.

Row 11: P6, [6-St RKC] twice, p6.

Row 12: K6, p12, k6.

Row 13: P4, 5-St RPC, 6-St LKC, 5-St LPC, p4.

Row 14: K4, p3, k2, p6, k2, p3, k4.

Row 15: P2, 5-St RPC, p2, k6, p2, 5-St LPC, p2.

Row 16: K2, p3, k4, p6, k4, p3, k2.

Repeat rows 1 – 16.

ENCLOSED CABLE – MAKE A SWATCH

Cast on 46 stitches.

Row 1 (RS): K3, p1, k3, p4, k6, p4, k3, p2, k12, p5, k3.

Row 2: K8, p12, k2, p3, k4, p6, k4, p3, k4.

Row 3: K3, p1, 5-St LPC, p2, k6, p2, 5-St RPC, p2, [6-St RKC] twice, p5, k3.

Row 4: K8, p12, k4, p3, k2, p6, k2, p3, k6.

Row 5: K3, p3, 5-St LPC, 6-St LKC, 5-St RPC, p2, 5-St RPC, 6-St LKC, 5-St LPC, p3, k3.

Row 6: K6, p3, k2, p6, k2, p3, k4, p12, k8.

Row 7: K3, p5, [6-St RKC] twice, p2, 5-St RPC, p2, k6, p2, 5-St LPC, p1, k3.

Row 8: K4, p3, k4, p6, k4, p3, k2, p12, k8.

Row 9: K3, p5, k3, 6-St LKC, k3, p2, k3, p4, k6, p4, k3, p1, k3.

Row 10: K4, p3, k4, p6, k4, p3, k2, p12, k8.

Row 11: K3, p5, [6-St RKC] twice, p2, 5-St LPC, p2, k6, p2, 5-St RPC, p1, k3.

Row 12: K6, p3, k2, p6, k2, p3, k4, p12, k8.

Row 13: K3, p3, 5-St RPC, 6-St LKC, 5-St LPC, p2, 5-St LPC, 6-St LKC, 5-St RPC, p3, k3.

Row 14: K8, p12, k4, p3, k2, p6, k2, p3, k6.

Row 15: K3, p1, 5-St RPC, p2, k6, p2, 5-St LPC, p2, [6-St RKC] twice, p5, k3.

Row 16: K8, p12, k2, p3, k4, p6, k4, p3, k4.

Row 17: K3, p1, k3, p4, k6, p4, k3, p2, k3, 6-St LKC, k3, p5, k3.

Row 18: K8, p12, k2, p3, k4, p6, k4, p3, k4.

Rows 19 – 32: Repeat rows 3 – 16.

Bind off all stitches in pattern.

	Knit on RS, purl on WS
	Purl on RS, knit on WS
	5-St RPC
	5-St LPC
	6-St RKC
	6-St LKC

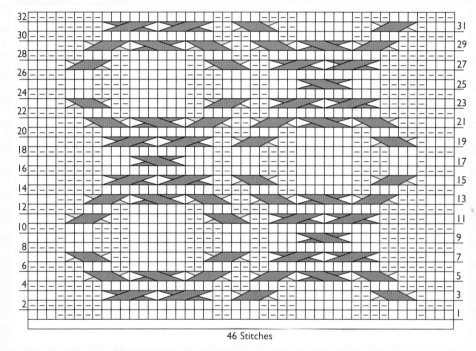

46 Stitches

DANCING CIRCLES CABLE

A series of simple cables combine to make this lively design. The middle section of 16 stitches, marked with heavy lines, is repeated until the desired width is reached. The sections outside the heavy lines are used only once to complete the side edges. The stitch count on the edges changes but the two sides combined always equal 8 stitches.

BASIC PATTERN

Multiple of 16 stitches plus 8 edge stitches

Directions related to the center 16-St Repeat section are in parentheses.

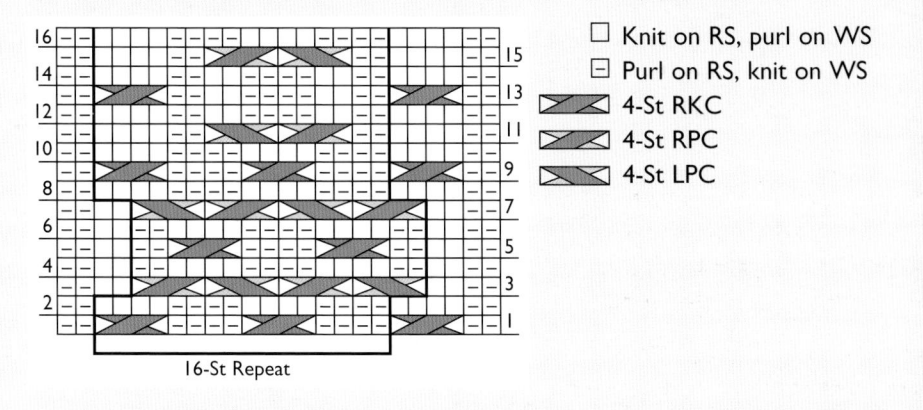

☐ Knit on RS, purl on WS

⊟ Purl on RS, knit on WS

▨ 4-St RKC

▨ 4-St RPC

▨ 4-St LPC

16-St Repeat

Row 1 (RS): P2, 4-St RKC, [p4, 4-St RKC] twice, p2.

Row 2: K2, [p4, k4] twice, p4, k2.

Row 3: P2, k2, [4-St LPC, 4-St RPC] twice, k2, p2.

Row 4: K2, p2, [k2, p4, k2] twice, p2, k2.

Row 5: P2, k2, [p2, 4-St RKC, p2] twice, k2, p2.

Row 6: K2, p2, [k2, p4, k2] twice, p2, k2.

Row 7: P2, k2, [4-St RPC, 4-St LPC] twice, p2, k2.

Row 8: K2, [p4, k4] twice, p4, k2.

Row 9: P2, 4-St RKC, [p4, 4-St RKC] twice, p2.

Row 10: K2, [p4, k4] twice, p4, k2.

Row 11: P2, k4, p2, 4-St RPC, 4-St LPC, p2, k4, p2.

Row 12: K2, p4, k2, p2, k4, p2, k2, p4, k2.

Row 13: P2, 4-St RKC, p2, k2, p4, k2, p2, 4-St RKC, p2.

Row 14: K2, p4, k2, p2, k4, p2, k2, p4, k2.

Row 15: P2, k4, p2, 4-St LPC, 4-St RPC, p2, k4, p2.

Row 16: K2, [p4, k4] twice, p4, k2.

Repeat rows 1 – 16.

DANCING CIRCLES CABLE – MAKE A SWATCH

The directions for the swatch are almost identical to the basic pattern even though it contains more stitches. In the case of the swatch, two center sections are combined and bordered with the edge pieces.

Cast on 40 stitches.

Row 1 (RS): K6, *p4, k4*; repeat from * to * until last 2 sts, k2.

Row 2: K2, *p4, k4*; repeat from * to * until last 6 sts, p4, k2.

Row 3: K2, 4-St RKC, *p4, 4-St RKC*; repeat from * to * until last 2 sts, k2.

Row 4: K2, *p4, k4*; rep from * to * until last 6 sts, p4, k2.

Row 5: K4, *4-St LPC, 4-St RPC*; repeat from * to * until last 4 sts, k4.

Row 6: K2, p2, *k2, p4, k2; repeat from * to * until last 4 sts, p2, k2.

Row 7: K4, *p2, 4-St RKC, p2*; repeat from * to * until last 4 sts, k4.

Row 8: Repeat row 6.

Row 9: K4, *4-St RPC, 4-St LPC*; repeat from * to * until last 4 sts, k4.

Row 10: Repeat row 4.

Rows 11 – 12: Repeat rows 3 – 4.

Row 13: K6, *p2, 4-St RPC, 4-St LPC, p2 k4*; repeat from * to * until last 2 sts, k2.

Row 14: K2, *p4, k2, p2, k4, p2, k2*; repeat from * to *until last 6 sts, p4, k2.

Row 15: K2, 4-St RKC, *p2, k2, p4, k2, p2, 4-St RKC*; repeat from * to * until last 2 sts, k2.

Row 16: Repeat row 14.

Row 17: K6, *p2, 4-St LPC, 4-St RPC, p2, k4*; repeat from * to *until last 2 sts, k2.

Row 18: Repeat row 4.

Rows 19 – 28: Repeat rows 3 – 12.

Bind off all stitches in pattern.

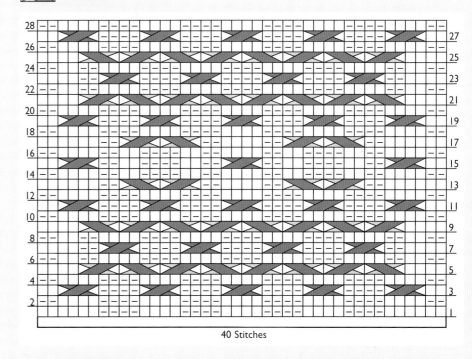

□ Knit on RS, purl on WS
⊟ Purl on RS, knit on WS
▨ 4-St RKC
▧ 4-St RPC
▨ 4-St LPC

40 Stitches

| # OVERSIZED PILLOW

The dancing circles cable is a natural choice to make a pillow. Chunky alpaca is knit using large needles so the project is finished quickly. This particular yarn is hand dyed and the color variation adds an unusual depth to the design.

FINISHED MEASUREMENTS
18" (45.7 cm) square after sewing
18" wide x 38" long (45.7 x 97cm) before sewing

GAUGE
13 stitches and 17 rows = 4" (10 cm) in stockinette stitch on larger needle
20 stitches and 19 rows = 4" (10 cm) in cable pattern

MATERIALS
Bulky weight hand-dyed alpaca yarn, approx 525 yd (480 m)

THE YARN USED FOR THIS PROJECT
Frog Tree Chunky Weight MultiTone Alpaca; 100% Alpaca;
    108 yd (100 m)/3.5 oz (100 g): 5 skeins, color Red #23

NEEDLES AND NOTIONS
Size 9 (6 mm) knitting needles or size necessary to obtain gauge
Size 10½ (6.5 mm) knitting needles
Cable needle
Yarn needle for weaving in ends
18" (45.7 cm) square pillow form
Three buttons, 1" (2.5 cm) diameter

SETUP ROWS

First, work a 6-row section with a garter stitch border. Several increases will set up your knitting to work the main section.

Using smaller needles, cast on 67 stitches.

Row 1 (RS): Knit.

Row 2: Knit.

Row 3: K3, *inc 1, k5 *; repeat from * to * until last 4 sts, inc 1, k3—78 sts.

Row 4: K2, p4, * k3, p4 *; repeat from * to * until last 2 sts, k2.

Change to larger needles.

Row 5: P2, 4-St RKC, *p3, 4-St RKC *; repeat from * to * until last 2 sts, p2.

Row 6: K2, p4, *k1, inc 1, k1, p4 *; repeat from * to * until last 2 sts, k2— 88 sts.

MAIN SECTION
PILLOW COVER CHART

☐ Knit on RS, purl on WS
⊟ Purl on RS, knit on WS
◨ 4-St RKC
◨ 4-St RPC
◨ 4-St LPC

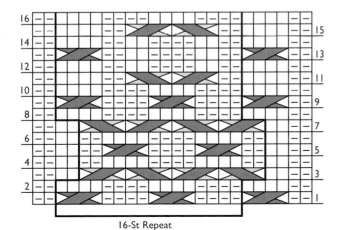

16-St Repeat

Repeat the Dancing Circles pattern over and over until your piece measures about 36" (91.4 cm) in length. If the piece is too short after the given number of rows, then work another repeat. Since the knitted fabric will be overlapped, it's ok to be longer; it's not ok to be shorter. To be absolutely certain that your knitting is long enough, measure it on the pillow. It should wrap around completely with an overlap of at least 2" (5.1 cm).

Row 1 (RS): P2, 4-St RKC, *p4, 4-St RKC*; repeat from * to * until last 2 sts, p2.

Row 2: K2, *p4, k4*; repeat from * to * until last 6 sts, p4, k2.

Row 3: P2, k2, *4-St LPC, 4-St RPC*; repeat from * to * until last 4 sts, k2, p2.

Row 4: K2, p2, *k2, p4, k2*; repeat from * to * until last 4 sts, p2, k2.

Row 5: P2, k2, *p2, 4-St RKC, p2*; repeat from * to * until last 4 sts, k2, p2.

Row 6: K2, p2, *k2, p4, k2*; repeat from * to * until last 4 sts, p2, k2.

Row 7: P2, k2, *4-St RPC, 4-St LPC*; repeat from * to * until last 4 sts, k2, p2.

Row 8: K2, *p4, k4*; repeat from * to * until last 6 sts, p4, k2.

Row 9: P2, 4-St RKC, *p4, 4-St RKC*; repeat from * to * until last 2 sts, p2.

Row 10: K2, *p4, k4*; repeat from * to * until last 6 sts, p4, k2.

Row 11: P2, k4, *p2, 4-St RPC, 4-St LPC, p2 k4*; repeat from * to * until last 2 sts, p2.

Row 12: K2, *p4, k2, p2, k4, p2, k2*; repeat from * to *until last 6 sts, p4, k2.

Row 13: P2, 4-St RKC, *p2, k2, p4, k2, p2, 4-St RKC*; repeat from * to *until last 2 sts, p2.

Row 14: K2, *p4, k2, p2, k4, p2, k2*; repeat from * to * until last 6 sts, p4, k2.

Row 15: P2, k4, *p2, 4-St LPC, 4-St RPC, p2, k4*; repeat from * to *until last 2 sts, p2.

Row 16: K2, *p4, k4*; repeat from * to * until last 6 sts, p4, k2.

Repeat rows 1 – 16 (10 more times), then work rows 1 – 9.

Finally, work a second garter stitch band containing some decreases and three buttonholes.

Row 1 (WS): K2, p4, *k1, k2tog, k1, p4 *; repeat from * to * until last 2 sts, k2 – 78 sts.

Row 2: P2, 4-St RKC, *p3, 4-St RKC; repeat from * to * until last 2 sts, p2.

Row 3: K3, k2tog, *k5, k2tog*; repeat from * to * until last 3 sts, k3 – 67 sts. Change to smaller needles.

Row 4 *(Make buttonholes):* [K15, k2tog, yo] 3 times, k16.

Row 5: Knit across.

Bind off all stitches in pattern.

FINISHING

- Using the tapestry needle, weave in all ends.

- If desired, lightly steam block using a steam iron on a wool setting. Don't let the iron actually touch the knitting.

- With right side of the knitting facing the right side of the pillow, wrap the strip around the pillow so the short ends overlap in the center of the pillow. Make sure that the finishing band with the buttonholes is touching the pillow with the other band on top (closest to you). Remember, you are working with the pillow cover inside out at this point. Without catching the pillow, pin each side in 5 or 6 places. Then gently remove the pillow form.

- Using yarn threaded on a yarn needle, sew the sides using a backstitch. The overlap will be in the center of the seam. When you get to this point, sew through all the layers, checking frequently that you are catching all three layers.

- Turn pillow cover right side out and mark button locations under the buttonholes. Sew on three buttons. If desired, use a small square of wool felt on the backside of the button so your stitches don't pull through the knitting.

- Insert pillow form and button closed.

DEPENDING ON YOUR personal knitting style and the size needle you use, you might find that you need to add extra rows in order to make your project to the same length. If this happens to you on the pillow, then you might need to sew your buttons on the cable section instead of the garter band in order to make the cover fit snugly on the pillow.

CHOOSING YARN FOR CABLE DESIGNS

Usually, cables are knit using smooth, light colored wool yarn; think of the traditional cream colored Aran Fisherman sweater. I love the look of traditional cables but since I own a yarn shop, I wanted to explore knitting cables from a diverse range of yarns. You'll find that some of the projects in this book, like the baby sweater and Journal Cover, use more traditional yarns. Other projects such as the Messenger Bag and the Boho Belt use smooth yarns made from unusual fibers such as hemp or sueded nylon. Several of the designs are a complete break from tradition, using two yarns knit together or multi-fiber yarns.

If you plan to knit a cable design from a multi-colored yarn or one with a 'bumpy' texture be sure and use a cable that is worked on a large scale. Either use large needles, such as for the Laptop Cover or use a boldly textural cable like the Butterfly Shawl. If you used hand-dyed yarns (which I adore) be sure and pick colors that are more subtle. Don't be afraid to experiment! Just remember that the emphasis should be as much on the cable as it is on the yarn.

GAUGE AND NEEDLE SIZE

Each of the projects in this book tells you what type of yarn and size of needle to use. The needle size is a recommendation only; it's just a starting point. The average knitter would probably use that needle but who says you're average?

If you want your project to turn out like those shown in the book then it is essential that you make a gauge swatch. Most knitters hate making gauge swatches but you will save yourself a lot of disappointment if you'll take a few moments to get the right needle size before you begin your project. Every project tells you what the gauge should be in stockinette stitch. Cast on the number of stitches specified and knit a few inches (NOT just a few rows). Measure the swatch from side to side. If the swatch is less than 4" (10 cm) wide, then use a larger needle. If it's wider than 4" (10 cm) then use a smaller needle. Don't try to change your personal style as a knitter (tight or loose); just change your needle size.

IRISH TWIST CABLE

Numerous small cables combine to create a classic Irish motif. It looks complicated but it's really easy. Be sure you pay attention to whether the small cables are knit crosses or purl crosses.

BASIC PATTERN
Multiple of 12 stitches with 4 edge stitches *(optional)*

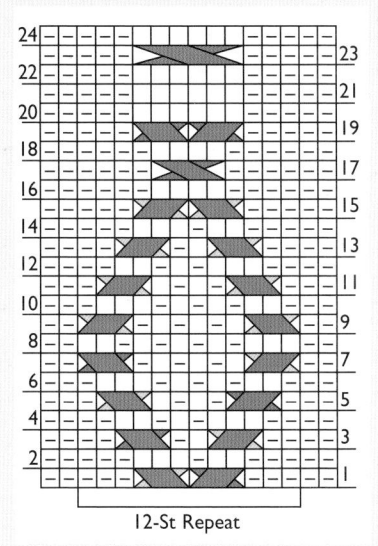

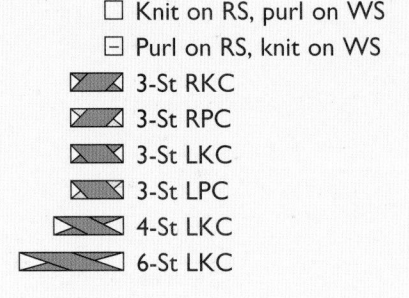

☐ Knit on RS, purl on WS

⊟ Purl on RS, knit on WS

▨ 3-St RKC

▨ 3-St RPC

▨ 3-St LKC

▨ 3-St LPC

▨ 4-St LKC

▨ 6-St LKC

12-St Repeat

Row 1 (RS): P5, 3-St RKC, 3-St LPC, p5.

Row 2: K5, p3, k1, p2, k5.

Row 3: P4, 3-St RPC, k1, p1, 3-St LKC, p4.

Row 4: K4, p2, k1, p1, k1, p3, k4.

Row 5: P3, 3-St RKC, [p1, k1] twice, 3-St LPC, p3.

Row 6: K3, p3, [k1, p1]twice, k1, p2, k3.

Row 7: P2, 3-St RPC, [k1, p1]3 times, 3-St LKC, p2.

Row 8: K2, p2, [k1, p1]4 times, p2, k2.

Row 9: P2, 3-St LPC, [k1, p1] 3 times, 3-St RPC, p2.

Row 10: K3, p3, [k1, p1] twice, k1, p2, k3.

Row 11: P3, 3-St LPC, [p1, k1] twice, 3-St RPC, p3.

Row 12: K4, p2, k1, p1, k1, p3, k4.

Row 13: P4, 3-St LPC, k1, p1, 3-St RPC, p4.

Row 14: K5, p3, k1, p2, k5.

Row 15: P5, 3-St LPC, 3-St RPC, p5.

Row 16: K6, p4, k6.

Row 17: P6, 4-St LKC, p6.

Row 18: K6, p4, k6.

Row 19: P5, 3-St RKC, 3-St LKC, p5.

Row 20: K5, p6, k5.

Row 21: P5, k6, p5.

Row 22: K5, p6, k5.

Row 23: P5, 6-St LKC, p5.

Row 24: K5, p6, k5.

Repeat rows 1 – 20.

Cast on 36 stitches.

Row 1 (RS): K3, [p5, k4, p5, k2] twice, k1.

Row 2: K1, p2, [k5, p4, k5, p2] twice, k1.

Row 3: K3, [p5, k4, p5, k2] twice, k1.

Row 4: K1, p2, [k5, p4, k5, p2] twice, k1.

Row 5: K3, [p5, 4-St LKC, p5, k2] twice, k1.

Row 6: K1, p2, [k5, p4, k5, p2] twice, k1.

Row 7: K3, [p4, 3-St RKC, 3-St LKC, p4, k2] twice, k1.

Row 8: K1, p2, [k4, p6, k4, p2] twice, k1.

Row 9: K3, [p4, k6, p4, k2] twice, k1.

Row 10: K1, p2, [k4, p6, k4, p2] twice, k1.

Row 11: K3, [p4, 6-St LKC, p4, k2] twice, k1.

Row 12: K1, p2, [k4, p6, k4, p2] twice, k1.

Row 13: K3, [p4, 3-St RKC, 3-St LPC, p4, k2] twice, k1.

Row 14: K1, p2, [k4, p3, k1, p2, k4, p2] twice, k1.

Row 15: K3, [p3, 3-St RPC, k1, p1, 3-St LKC, p3, k2] twice, k1.

Row 16: K1, p2, [k3, p2, k1, p1, k1, p3, k3, p2] twice, k1.

Row 17: K3, *p2, 3-St RKC, [p1, k1] twice, 3-St LKC, p2, k2*; repeat from * to *, k1.

Row 18: K1, p2, *k2, p3, [k1, p1] twice, k1, p2, k2, p2*; repeat from * to *, k1.

Row 19: K3, *p1, 3-St RPC, [k1, p1] 3 times, 3-St LKC, p1, k2*; repeat from * to *, k1.

Row 20: K1, *p2, k1, p2, [k1, p1] 4 times, p2, k1*; repeat from * to *, p2, k1.

Row 21: K3, *p1, 3-St LPC, [k1, p1] 3 times, 3-St RPC, p1, k2*; repeat from * to *, k1.

Row 22: K1, p2, *k2, p3, [k1, p1] twice, k1, p2, k2, p2*; repeat from * to *, k1.

Row 23: K3, *p2, 3-St LPC, [p1, k1] twice, 3-St RPC, p2, k2*; repeat from * to *, k1.

Row 24: K1, p2, [k3, p2, k1, p1, k1, p3, k3, p2] twice, k1.

Row 25: K3, [p3, 3-St LPC, k1, p1, 3-St RPC, p3, k2] twice, k1.

Row 26: K1, p2, [k4, p3, k1, p2, k4, p2] twice, k1.

Row 27: K3, [p4, 3-St LPC, 3-St RPC, p4, k2] twice, k1.

Row 28: K1, p2, [k5, p4, k5, p2] twice, k1.

Rows 29 – 36: Repeat rows 5 – 12.

Row 37: K3, [p4, k6, p4, k2] twice, k1.

Row 38: K1, p2, [k4, p6, k4, p2] twice, k1.

Row 39: K3, [p4, k6, p4, k2] twice, k1.

Bind off all stitches in pattern.

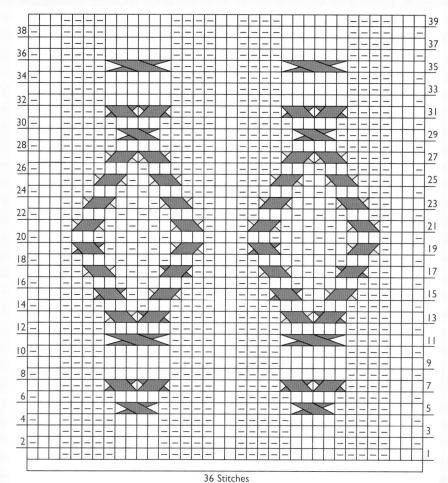

☐ Knit on RS, purl on WS
⊟ Purl on RS, knit on WS
▨ 3-St RKC
▨ 3-St RPC
▨ 3-St LKC
▨ 3-St LPC
▤ 4-St LKC
▤ 6-St LKC

36 Stitches

CLASSIC ARAN DIAMOND CABLE

A diamond enclosing double seed stitch is combined
with a bobble to make this classic cable. Because it includes
so many details, the swatch for this cable is huge.
Why not make two of them and create a small bag
by seaming them together on three sides?

BASIC PATTERN
Multiple of 13 stitches with 4 edge stitches *(optional)*

☐ Knit on RS, purl on WS
⊟ Purl on RS, knit on WS
⊡ Make Bobble (MB)
3-St RPC
3-St LPC
5-St RC

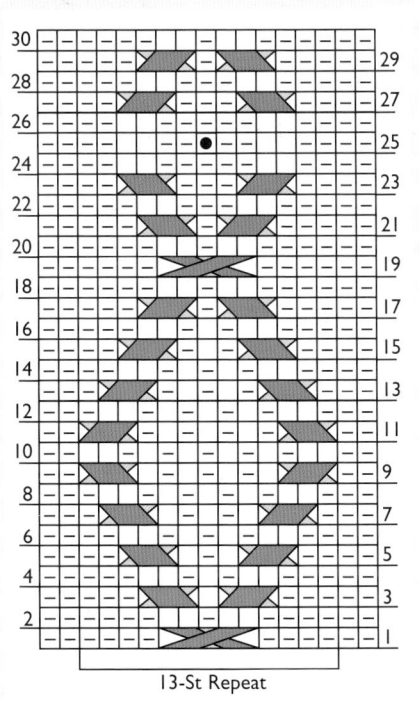

13-St Repeat

Row 1 (RS): P6, 5-St RC, p6.
Row 2: K6, p2, k1, p2, k6.
Row 3: P5, 3-St RPC, k1, 3-St LPC, p5.
Row 4: K5, p2, k1, p1, k1, p2, k5.
Row 5: P4, 3-St RPC, k1, p1, k1, 3-St LPC, p4.
Row 6: K4, p2, [k1, p1] twice, k1, p2, k4.
Row 7: P3, 3-St RPC, [k1, p1] twice, k1, 3-St LPC, p3.
Row 8: K3, p2, [k1, p1] 3 times, k1, p2, k3.
Row 9: P2, 3-St RPC, [k1, p1] 3 times, k1, 3-St LPC, p2.
Row 10: K2, p2, [k1, p1] 4 times, k1, p2, k2.
Row 11: P2, 3-St LPC, [p1, k1] 3 times, p1, 3-St RPC, p2.
Row 12: K3, p2, [k1, p1] 3 times, k1, p2, k3.
Row 13: P3, 3-St LPC, [p1, k1] twice, p1, 3-St RPC, p3.
Row 14: K4, p2, [k1, p1] twice, k1, p2, k4.
Row 15: P4, 3-St LPC, p1, k1, p1, 3-St RPC, p4.
Row 16: K5, p2, k1, p1, k1, p2, k5.
Row 17: P5, 3-St LPC, p1, 3-St RPC, p6.
Row 18: K6, p2, k1, p2, k6.
Row 19: P6, 5-St RC, p6.
Row 20: K6, p2, k1, p2, k6.
Row 21: P5, 3-St RPC, p1, 3-St LPC, p5.
Row 22: K5, p2, k3, p2, k5.
Row 23: P4, 3-St RPC, p3, 3-St LPC, p4.
Row 24: K4, p2, k5, p2, k4.

Row 25: P4, k2, p2, MB, p2, k2, p4.
Row 26: K4, p2, k5, p2, k4.
Row 27: P4, 3-St LPC, p3, 3-St RPC, p4.
Row 28: K5, p2, k3, p2, k5.
Row 29: P5, 3-St LPC, p1, 3-St RPC, p5.
Row 30: K6, p2, k1, p2, k6.
Repeat rows 1 – 30.

CLASSIC ARAN DIAMOND CABLE –

□ Knit on RS, purl on WS
⊟ Purl on RS, knit on WS
◉ Make Bobble (MB)
▨ 3-St RPC
▨ 3-St LPC
⧓ 5-St RC

MAKE A SWATCH

Cast on 42 stitches.

Row 1 (RS): [K1, p1] twice, k1, p6, k5, p10, k5, p6 [k1, p1] twice, k1.

Row 2: [P1, k1] twice, p1, k6, p5, k10, p5, k6, [p1, k1] twice, p1.

Row 3: [P1, k1] twice, p7, k5, p10, k5, p7, [k1, p1] twice.

Row 4: [K1, p1] twice, k7, p5, k10, p5, k7, [p1, k1] twice.

Rows 5 – 8: Repeat rows 1 – 4.

Row 9: [K1, p1] twice, k1, p6, 5-St RC, p10, 5-St RC, p6, [k1, p1] twice, k1.

Row 10: [P1, k1] twice, p1, k6, p2, k1, p2, k10, p2, k1, p2, k6, [p1, k1] twice, p1.

Row 11: [P1, k1] twice, p6, 3-St RPC, k1, 3-St LPC, p8, 3-St RPC, k1, 3-St LPC, p6, [k1, p1] twice.

Row 12: [K1, p1] twice, k6, p2, k1, p1, k1, p2, k8, p2, k1, p1, k1, p2, k6, [p1, k1] twice.

Row 13: [K1, p1] twice, k1, p4, 3-St RPC, k1, p1, k1, 3-St LPC, p6, 3-St RPC, k1, p1, k1, 3-St LPC, p4, [k1, p1] twice, k1.

Row 14: [P1, k1] twice, p1, k4, p2, [k1, p1] twice, k1, p2, k6, p2, [k1, p1] twice, k1, p2, k4, [p1, k1] twice, p1.

Row 15: [P1, k1] twice, p4, 3-St RPC, [k1, p1] twice, k1, 3-St LPC, p4, 3-St RPC, [k1, p1] twice, k1, 3-St LPC, p4, [k1, p1] twice.

Row 16: [K1, p1] twice, k4, p2, [k1, p1] 3 times, k1, p2, k4, p2, [k1, p1] 3 times, k1, p2, k4, [p1, k1] twice.

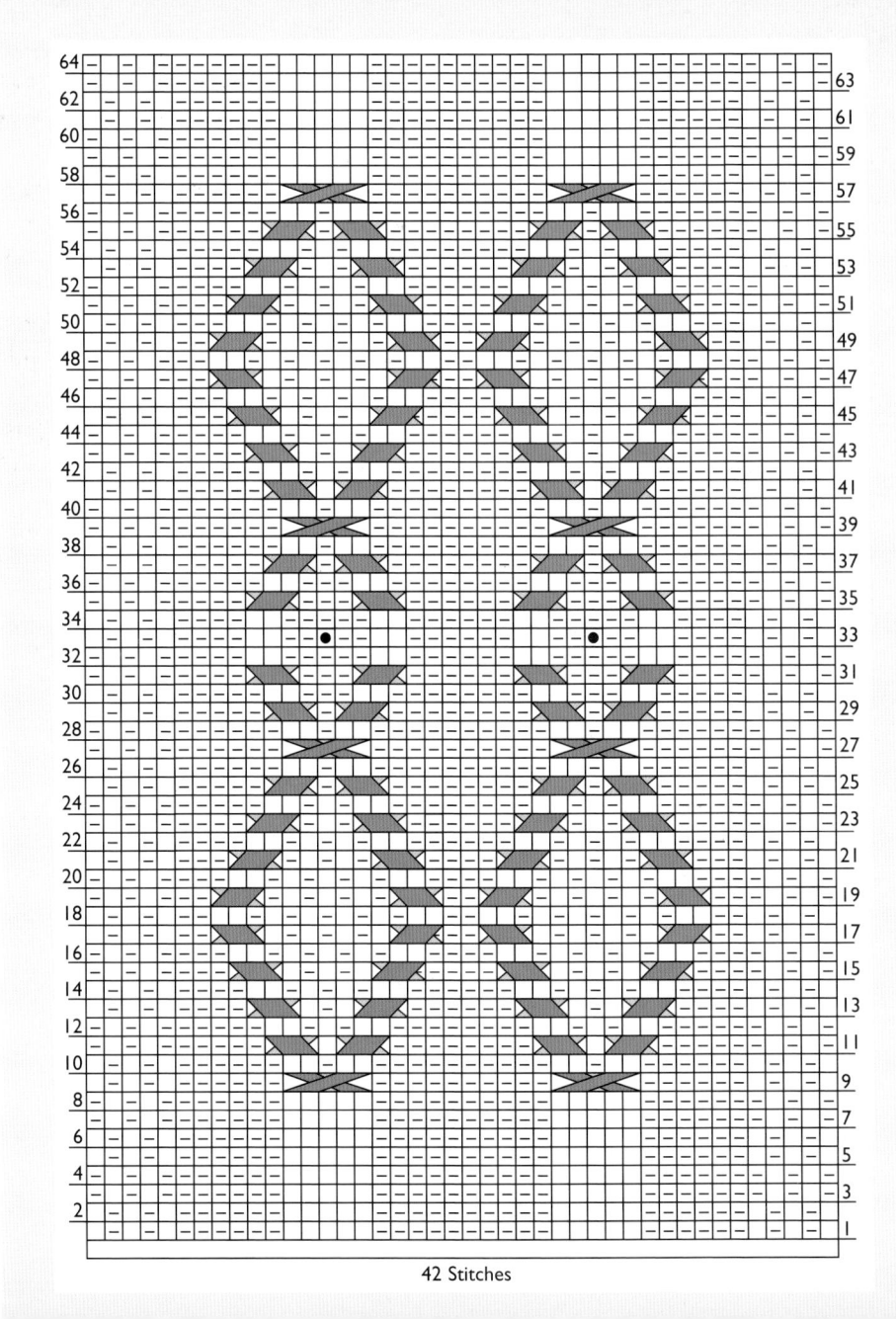

42 Stitches

Row 17: [K1, p1] twice, k1, p2, 3-St RPC, [k1, p1] 3 times, k1, 3-St LPC, p2, 3-St RPC, [k1, p1] 3 times, k1, 3-St LPC, p2, [k1, p1] twice, k1.

Row 18: [P1, k1] twice, p1, k2, p2, [k1, p1] 4 times, k1, p2, k2, p2, [k1, p1] 4 times, k1, p2, k2, [p1, k1] twice, p1.

Row 19: [P1, k1] twice, p3, 3-St LPC, [p1, k1] 3 times, p1, 3-St RPC, p2, 3-St LPC, [p1, k1] 3 times, p1, 3-St RPC, p3, [k1, p1] twice.

Row 20: [K1, p1] twice, k4, p2, [k1, p1] 3 times, k1, p2, k4, p2, [k1, p1] (3 times), k1, p2, k4, [p1, k1] twice.

Row 21: [K1, p1] twice, k1, p3, 3-St LPC, [p1, k1] twice, p1, 3-St RPC, p4, 3-St LPC, [p1, k1] twice, p1, 3-St RPC, p3, [k1, p1] twice, k1.

Row 22: [P1, k1] twice, p1, k4, p2, [k1, p1] twice, k1, p2, k6, p2, [k1, p1] twice, k1, p2, k4, [p1, k1] twice, p1.

Row 23: [P1, k1] twice, p5, 3-St LPC, p1, k1, p1, 3-St RPC, p6, 3-St LPC, p1, k1, p1, 3-St RPC, p5, [k1, p1] twice.

Row 24: [K1, p1] twice, k6, p2, k1, p1, k1, p2, k8, p2, k1, p1, k1, p2, k6, [p1, k1] twice.

Row 25: [K1, p1] twice, k1, p5, 3-St LPC, p1, 3-St RPC, p8, 3-St LPC, p1, 3-St RPC, p5, [k1, p1] twice, k1.

Row 26: [P1, k1] twice, p1, k6, p2, k1, p2, k10, p2, k1, p2, k6, [p1, k1] twice, p1.

Row 27: [P1, k1] twice, p7, 5-St RC, p10, 5-St RC, p7, [k1, p1] twice.

Row 28: [K1, p1] twice, k7, p2, k1, p2, k10, p2, k1, p2, k7, [p1, k1] twice.

Row 29: [K1, p1] twice, k1, p5, 3-St RPC, p1, 3-St LPC, p8, 3-St RPC, p1, 3-St LPC, p5, [k1, p1] twice, k1.

Row 30: [P1, k1] twice, p1, k5, p2, k3, p2, k8, p2, k3, p2, k5, [p1, k1] twice, p1.

Row 31: [P1, k1] twice, p5, 3-St RPC, p3, 3-St LPC, p6, 3-St RPC, p3, 3-St LPC, p5, [k1, p1] twice.

Row 32: [K1, p1] twice, k5, p2, k5, p2, k6, p2, k5, p2, k5, [p1, k1] twice.

Row 33: [K1, p1] twice, k1, p4, k2, p2, MB, p2, k2, p6, k2, p2, MB, p2, k2, p4, [k1, p1] twice, k1.

Row 34: [P1, k1] twice, p1, k4, p2, k5, p2, k6, p2, k5, p2, k4, [p1, k1] twice, p1.

Row 35: [P1, k1] twice, p5, 3-St LPC, p3, 3-St RPC, p6, 3-St LPC, p3, 3-St RPC, p5, [k1, p1] twice.

Row 36: [K1, p1] twice, k6, p2, k3, p2, k8, p2, k3, p2, k6, [p1, k1] twice.

Row 37: [K1, p1] twice, k1, p5, 3-St LPC, p1, 3-St RPC, p8, 3-St LPC, p1, 3-St RPC, p5, [k1, p1] twice, k1.

Row 38: [P1, k1] twice, p1, k6, p2, k1, p2, k10, p2, k1, p2, k6, [p1, k1] twice, p1.

Row 39: [P1, k1] twice, p7, 5-St RC, p10, 5-St RC, p7, [k1, p1] twice.

Row 40: [K1, p1] twice, k7, p2, k1, p2, k10, p2, k1, p2, k7, [p1, k1] twice.

Row 41: [K1, p1] twice, k1, p5, 3-St RPC, k1, 3-St LPC, p8, 3-St RPC, p1, 3-St LPC, p5, [k1, p1] twice, k1.

Row 42: [P1, k1] twice, p1, k5, p2, k1, p1, k1, p2, k8, p2, k1, p1, k1, p2, k5, [p1, k1] twice, p1.

Row 43: [P1, k1] twice, p5, 3-St RPC, k1, p1, k1, 3-St LPC, p6, 3-St RPC, k1, p1, k1, 3-St LPC, p5, [k1, p1] twice.

Row 44: [K1, p1] twice, k5, p2, [k1, p1] twice, k1, p2, k6, p2, [k1, p1] twice, k1, p2, k5, [p1, k1] twice.

Row 45: [K1, p1] twice, k1, p3, 3-St RPC, [k1, p1] twice, k1, 3-St LPC, p4, 3-St RPC, [k1, p1] twice, k1, 3-St LPC, p3, [k1, p1] twice, k1.

Row 46: [P1, k1] twice, p1, k3, p2, [k1, p1] 3 times, k1, p2, k4, p2, [k1, p1] 3 times, k1, p2, k3, [p1, k1] twice, p1.

Row 47: [P1, k1] twice, p3, 3-St RPC, [k1, p1] 3 times, k1, 3-St LPC, p2, 3-St RPC, [k1, p1] 3 times, k1, 3-St LPC, p3, [k1, p1] twice.

Row 48: [K1, p1] twice, k3, p2, [k1, p1] 4 times, k1, p2, k2, p2, [k1, p1] 4 times, k1, p2, k3, [p1, k1] twice.

Row 49: [K1, p1] twice, k1, p2, 3-St LPC, [p1, k1] 3 times, p1, 3-St RPC, p2, 3-St LPC, [p1, k1] (3 times), p1, 3-St RPC, p2, [k1, p1] twice, k1.

Row 50: [P1, k1] twice, p1, k3, p2, [k1, p1] 3 times, k1, p2, k4, p2, [k1, p1] 3 times, k1, p2, k3, [p1, k1] twice, p1.

Row 51: [P1, k1] twice, p4, 3-St LPC, [p1, k1] twice, p1, 3-St RPC, p4, 3-St LPC, [p1, k1] twice, p1, 3-St RPC, p4, [k1, p1] twice.

Row 52: [K1, p1] twice, k5, p2, [k1, p1] twice, k1, p2, k6, p2, [k1, p1] twice, k1, p2, k5, [p1, k1] twice.

Row 53: [K1, p1] twice, k1, p4, 3-St LPC, p1, k1, p1, 3-St RPC, p6, 3-St LPC, p1, k1, p1, 3-St RPC, p4, [k1, p1] twice, k1.

Row 54: [P1, k1] twice, p1, k5, p2, k1, p1, k1, p2, k8, p2, k1, p1, k1, p2, k5, [p1, k1] twice, p1.

Row 55: [P1, k1] twice, p6, 3-St LPC, p1, 3-St RPC, p8, 3-St LPC, p1, 3-St RPC, p6, [k1, p1] twice.

Row 56: [K1, p1] twice, k7, p2, k1, p2, k10, p2, k1, p2, k7, [p1, k1] twice.

Row 57: [K1, p1] twice, k1, p6, 5-St RC, p10, 5-St RC, p6, [k1, p1] twice, k1.

Rows 58 – 64: Repeat rows 2 – 8.
Bind off all stitches in pattern.

JOURNAL COVER WITH RIBBON TIES

Turn an ordinary spiral notebook into a charming journal. As a finishing touch, ribbon is woven into the space created by the cable crossings.

FINISHED MEASUREMENTS

10" wide x 21" long (25.4 x 53.3 cm)

GAUGE

18 stitches and 23 rows = 4" (10 cm) in stockinette stitch with larger needle
22 stitches and 23 rows = 4" (10 cm) in cable pattern

MATERIALS

Medium weight cotton yarn, approx 185 y (168 m)

THE YARN USED FOR THIS PROJECT

Rowan All Seasons Cotton; 60% cotton, 40% acrylic, 98 yd (90 m)/1.75 oz
    (50 g); 2 skeins, color Jazz #185

NEEDLES AND NOTIONS

Size 5 (3.75 mm) knitting needles or size necessary to obtain gauge.
Size 7 (4.5 mm) knitting needles
Cable needle
Yarn needle for weaving in ends
2 yd (2 m) ribbon, ⅜" (1 cm) wide

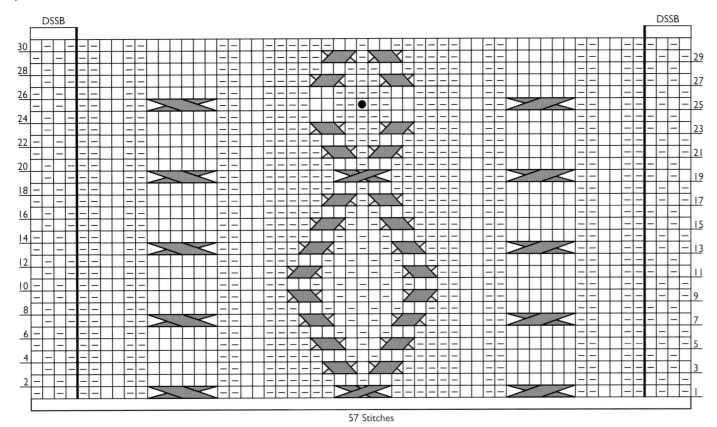

57 Stitches

☐ Knit on RS, purl on WS
⊟ Purl on RS, knit on WS
▣ Make Bobble (MB)
▧ 3-St RPC
▧ 3-St LPC
▧ 5-St RC
▧ 6-St RKC
▧ 6-St LKC

Double Seed Stitch Border (DSSB) – worked over four stitches on each side

Row I (RS): PI, kI, pI, kI, [work chart], kI, pI, kI, pI.

Row 2: KI, pI, kI, pI, [work chart], pI, kI, pI, kI.

Row 3: KI, pI, kI, pI, [work chart], pI, kI, pI, kI.

Row 4: PI, kI, pI, kI, [work chart], kI, pI, kI, pI.

BEGINNING SECTION

First you will knit a short garter stitch section (knit all rows). This will become the flap that folds to the inside of the journal. At the very end of the garter stitch rows, you will set up your knitting to make the transition to the front cover. Also note that several increases are called for on the last few rows of this section.

Using smaller needle, cast on 44 stitches.

Rows 1 – 20: Knit all stitches (Garter stitch).

Row 21 (RS): K2, *inc, k9*; repeat from * to * until last 2 stitches, inc, k1—49 sts.

Change to larger needles and work as follows:

Row 22: P1, k1, p1, k3, p2, k2, p4, k2, p2, k5, p3, k5, p2, k2, p4, k2, p2, k3, p1, k1, p1.

Row 23: K1, p1, k1, p3, k2, p2, k2, M1, k1, M1, k1, p2, k2, p5, k1, M1, k1, M1, k1, p5, k2, p2, k2, M1, k1, M1, k1, p2, k2, p3, k1, p1, k1—55 sts.

Row 24: K1, p1, k1, p1, k2, p2, k2, p6, k2, p2, k2, inc, k2, p5, k2, inc, k2, p2, k2, p6, k2, p2, k2, k1, p1, k1, p1—57 sts.

MAIN SECTION

The main section is the outside of the journal cover. You will begin and end each row with four stitches worked in the Double Seed Stitch Border following the directions above. These stitches are shown on the chart but will only be referred to in the directions as DSSB. Begin row 1 of the DSSB at the same time as row 1 of the cable chart but continue repeating the DSSB every four rows (the cable chart is knit for 30 rows before repeating).

Row 1 (RS): DSSB, p2, k2, p2, 6-St RKC, p2, k2, p6, 5-St RC, p6, k2, p2, 6-St LKC, p2, k2, p2, DSSB.

Row 2: DSSB, k2, p2, k2, p6, k2, p2, k6, p2, k1, p2, k6, p2, k2, p6, k2, p2, k2, DSSB.

Row 3: DSSB, p2, k2, p2, k6, p2, k2, p5, 3-St RPC, k1, 3-St LPC, p5, k2, p2, k6, p2, k2, p2, DSSB.

Row 4: DSSB, k2, p2, k2, p6, k2, p2, k5, p2, k1, p1, k1, p2, k5, p2, k2, p6, k2, p2, k2, DSSB.

Row 5: DSSB, p2, k2, p2, k6, p2, k2, p4, 3-St RPC, k1, p1, k1, 3-St LPC, p4, k2, p2, k6, p2, k2, p2, DSSB.

Row 6: DSSB, k2, p2, k2, p6, k2, p2, k4, p2, [k1, p1] twice, k1, p2, k4, p2, k2, p6, k2, p2, k2, DSSB.

Row 7: DSSB, p2, k2, p2, 6-St RKC, p2, k2, p3, 3-St RPC, [k1, p1] twice, k1, 3-St LPC, p3, k2, p2, 6-St LKC, p2, k2, p2, DSSB.

Row 8: DSSB, k2, p2, k2, p6, k2, p2, k3, p2, [k1, p1] 3 times, k1, p2, k3, p2, k2, p6, k2, p2, k2, DSSB.

Row 9: DSSB, p2, k2, p2, k6, p2, k2, p2, 3-St RPC, [k1, p1] 3 times, k1, 3-St LPC, p2, k2, p2, k6, p2, k2, p2, DSSB.

Row 10: DSSB, k2, p2, k2, p6, k2, p2, k2, p2, [k1, p1] 4 times, k1, p2, k2, p2, p6, k2, p2, k2, DSSB.

Row 11: DSSB, p2, k2, p2, k6, p2, k2, p2, 3-St LPC, [p1, k1] 3 times, p1, 3-St RPC, p2, k2, p2, k6, p2, k2, p2, DSSB.

Row 12: DSSB, k2, p2, k2, p6, k2, p2, k3, p2, [k1, p1] 3 times, k1, p2, k3, p2, k2, p6, k2, p2, k2, DSSB.

Row 13: DSSB, p2, k2, p2, 6-St RKC, p2, k2, p3, 3-St LPC, [p1, k1] twice, p1, 3-St RPC, p3, k2, p2, 6-St LKC, p2, k2, p2, DSSB.

Row 14: DSSB, k2, p2, k2, p6, k2, p2, k4, p2, [k1, p1] twice, k1, p2, k4, p2, k2, p6, k2, p2, k2, DSSB.

Row 15: DSSB, p2, k2, p2, k6, p2, k2, p4, 3-St LPC, p1, k1, p1, 3-St RPC, p4, k2, p2, k6, p2, k2, p2, DSSB.

Row 16: DSSB, k2, p2, k2, p6, k2, p2, k5, p2, k1, p1, k1, p2, k5, p2, k2, p6, k2, p2, k2, DSSB.

Row 17: DSSB, p2, k2, p2, k6, p2, k2, p5, 3-St LPC, p1, 3-St RPC, p5, k2, p2, k6, p2, k2, p2, DSSB.

Row 18: DSSB, k2, p2, k2, p6, k2, p2, k6, p2, k1, p2, k6, p2, k2, p6, k2, p2, k2, DSSB.

Row 19: DSSB, p2, k2, p2, 6-St RKC, p2, k2, p6, 5-St RC, p6, k2, p2, 6-St LKC, p2, k2, p2, DSSB.

Row 20: DSSB, k2, p2, k2, p6, k2, p2, k6, p2, k1, p2, k6, p2, k2, p6, k2, p2, k2, DSSB.

Row 21: DSSB, p2, k2, p2, k6, p2, k2, p5, 3-St RPC, p1, 3-St LPC, p5, k2, p2, k6, p2, k2, p2, DSSB.

Row 22: DSSB, k2, p2, k2, p6, k2, p2, k5, p2, k3, p2, k5, p2, k2, p6, k2, p2, k2, DSSB.

Row 23: DSSB, p2, k2, p2, k6, p2, k2, p4, 3-St RPC, p3, 3-St LPC, p4, k2, p2, k6, p2, k2, p2, DSSB.
Row 24: DSSB, k2, p2, k2, p6, k2, p2, k4, p2, k5, p2, k4, p2, k2, p6, k2, p2, k2, DSSB.
Row 25: DSSB, p2, k2, p2, 6-St RKC, p2, k2, p4, k2, p2, MB, p2, k2, p4, k2, p2, 6-St LKC, p2, k2, p2, DSSB.
Row 26: DSSB, k2, p2, k2, p6, k2, p2, k4, p2, k5, p2, k4, p2, k2, p6, k2, p2, k2, DSSB.
Row 27: DSSB, p2, k2, p2, k6, p2, k2, p4, 3-St LPC, p3, 3-St RPC, p4, k2, p2, k6, p2, k2, p2, DSSB.
Row 28: DSSB, k2, p2, k2, p6, k2, p2, k5, p2, k3, p2, k5, p2, k2, p6, k2, p2, k2, DSSB.
Row 29: DSSB, p2, k2, p2, k6, p2, k2, p5, 3-St LPC, p1, 3-St RPC, p5, k2, p2, k6, p2, k2, p2, DSSB.
Row 30: DSSB, k2, p2, k2, p6, k2, p2, k6, p2, k1, p2, k6, p2, k2, p6, k2, p2, k2, DSSB.
Rows 31 – 48: Repeat rows 1 – 18.
Rows 49 – 97: Repeat rows 1 – 30 (once), then rows 1 – 19.

ENDING SECTION

The ending section is a mirror image of the beginning section. You'll finish the last few rows on the front, working several decreases. Then the second inside flap is completed in garter stitch.

Row 1 (WS): K1, p1, k1, p1, k2, p2, k2, p6, k2, p2, k2, k2tog, k2, p5, k2, k2tog, k2, p2, k2, p6, k2, p2, k2, p1, k1, p1, k1—55 stitches.
Row 2: K1, p1, k1, p3, k2, p2, k2, [k2tog] (twice), p2, k2, p5, k1, [k2tog] twice, p5, k2, p2, k2, [k2tog] (twice), p2, k2, p3, k1, p1, k1—49 stitches.
Row 3: P1, k1, p1, k3, p2, k2, p4, k2, p2, k5, p3, k5, p2, k2, p4, k2, p2, k3, p1, k1, p1.
Change to smaller needles and continue knitting as follows:
Row 4: K2, *k2tog, k9*; repeat from * to * until last 3 stitches, k2tog, k1—44 stitches.
Rows 5 – 24: Knit all stitches (Garter stitch).
Bind off all stitches. Using the yarn needle, weave in all ends.

BLOCKING

You need to block the knitting so that the cable section is as wide from selvedge to selvedge as the spiral binding or spine of the journal.

Lay the journal cover on your ironing board or a blocking board. Pin one selvedge edge in a straight line pinning just the cable section. The beginning and ending garter sections will pull in a bit and be narrower than the cable section because they haven't been pinned. Using the journal as a guide, gently stretch the cable section from side to side (selvedge to selvedge) until the width is the same as the spine. As you stretch, pin along the edge. Using a steam iron allow steam to thoroughly penetrate the cable section of the cover. Allow the cover to dry while pinned to the board.

ASSEMBLY

After drying, remove pins from cover. The garter stitch bands at the beginning and end of the knitting form the flaps that fold to the inside of the journal and keep the cover in place. With right sides together, fold the flaps back with the crease just along the line where the garter stitch ended and the cable design began. Create a seam along the selvedge edge joining the garter flap to the front. Join with whipstitch using a yarn needle threaded with the same yarn used for knitting the cover. Turn flaps right side out so that wrong sides are together. Weave in all ends.

Cut two pieces of ribbon to a length of one yard (one meter) each. Weave the ribbon in and out of the six-stitch basic cable on both sides of the cover. Insert notebook covers into flaps, finger creasing the folded edge. It may be necessary to use some double stick carpet tape to secure the flap on the inside of the journal. In addition, if the cover pulls in a bit by the spine, then use more tape.

CABLES AND LACE CABLE

A simple lace stitch panel is combined with a cable to create a pretty and feminine design. The backside of this cable is attractive and it works well in a variety of yarns, especially hand-dyed yarns.

BASIC PATTERN
Multiple of 8 stitches with 4 edge stitches *(optional)*

☐ Knit on RS, purl on WS
⊟ Purl on RS, knit on WS
☒ K2tog in knit stitches; P2tog in purl stitches
☑ Yarn Over (yo)
▨ 4-St RKC

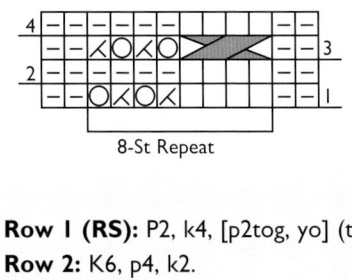

8-St Repeat

Row 1 (RS): P2, k4, [p2tog, yo] (twice), p2.
Row 2: K6, p4, k2.
Row 3: P2, 4-ST RKC, [yo, p2tog] (twice), p2.
Row 4: K6, p4, k2.
Repeat rows 1 – 4.

CABLES AND LACE – MAKE A SWATCH

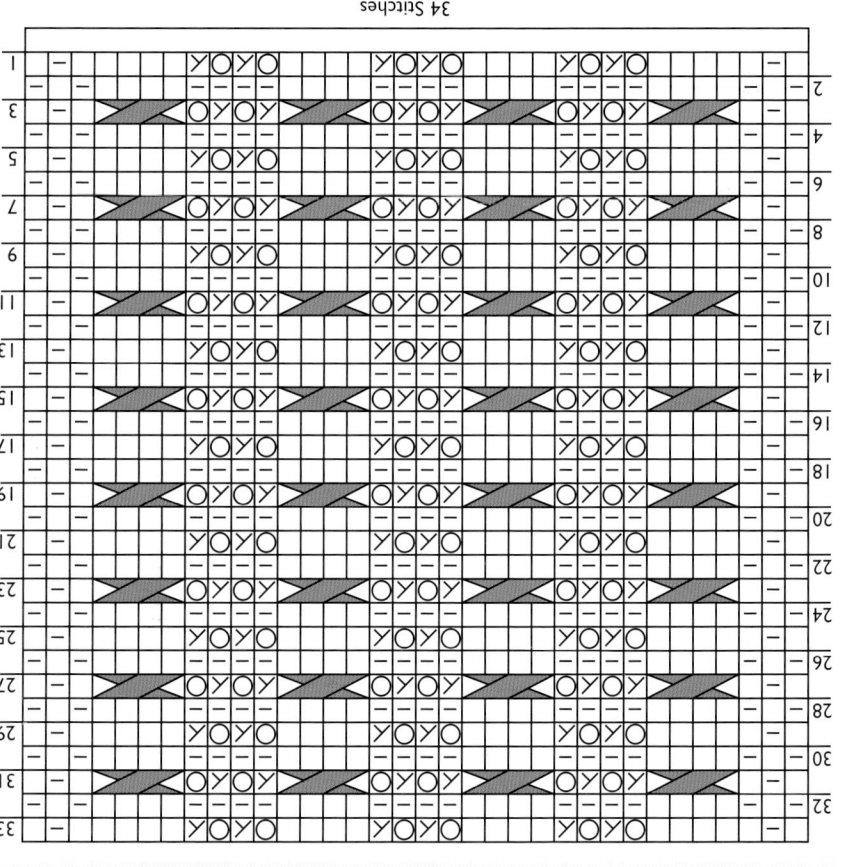

34 Stitches

Knit on RS, purl on WS

Legend:
- ☐ Knit on RS, purl on WS
- ⊟ Purl on RS, knit on WS
- ⊠ K2tog in knit stitches; P2tog in purl stitches
- ⊙ Yarn Over (yo)
- 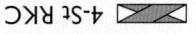 4-St RKC

Cast on 34 stitches.

Row 1 (RS): K1, p1, k5, [p2tog, yo, p2tog, k4] 3 times, k1, p1, k1.

Row 2: K1, p1, k1, p4, [k4, p4] 3 times, k1, p1, k1.

Row 3: K1, p1, k1, [4-St RKC, yo, p2tog, yo, p2tog] 3 times, 4-St RKC,k1, p1,k1.

Row 4: K1, p1, k1, p4, [k4, p4] 3 times, k1, p1, k1.

Rows 5 – 32: Repeat rows 1 – 4 (7 times more).

Row 33: K1, p1, k5, [p2tog, yo, p2tog, k4] 3 times, k1, p1, k1.

Bind off all stitches in pattern.

CABLES AND LACE SCARF

Hand-painted luxury yarn works beautifully with this easy cable. The lace panels keep the knitting lightweight and the scarf drapes beautifully. Also, the design looks attractive on both sides.

FINISHED MEASUREMENTS
7½" wide x 56" long (19.1 x 142 cm)

GAUGE
17 stitches and 24 rows = 4" (10 cm) in stockinette stitch
22 stitches and 22 rows = 4" (10 cm) in cable pattern

MATERIALS
Medium weight multi fiber yarn, approx 370 yd (338 m)

THE YARN USED FOR THIS PROJECT
Artyarns Silk Rhapsody Glitter; 50% silk, 50% kid mohair, trace of lurex;
    260 yd (238 m)/3.5 oz (100 g): 2 hanks, Light Blue color #123

NEEDLES AND NOTIONS
Size 8 (5 mm) needles or size necessary to obtain gauge
Cable needle
Yarn needle for weaving in ends

In order to make the cast-on and bound-off edges of the scarf lay flat, a few different rows are worked at the beginning and end. This will increase the stitches at the beginning and decrease the stitches at the end.

BEGINNING SECTION

CAST ON 37 STITCHES.

Row 1 (RS): K1, yo, p2tog, k3, *[p2tog, yo] twice, k3 *; repeat from * to * until last 3 stitches, p2tog, yo, k1.

Row 2: K3, *p1, inc, p1, k4*; repeat from * to * until last 6 stitches, p1, inc, p1, k3—42 sts. (Note that increases are worked in purl stitches.)

MAIN SECTION

Follow the Scarf Chart below.

Row 3: K1, yo, p2tog, 4-ST RKC, *[yo, p2tog] (twice), 4-ST RKC *; repeat from * to * until last 3 stitches, p2tog, yo, k1.

Row 4: K3, *p4, k4*; repeat from * to * until last 7 stitches, p4, k3.

Row 5: K1, yo, p2tog, k4, *[p2tog, yo] (twice), k4*; repeat from * to * until last 3 stitches, p2tog, yo, k1.

Row 6: K3, *p4, k4*; repeat from * to * until last 7 stitches, p4, k3.

Repeat rows 3 – 6 until scarf measures about 55½" (141 cm) or desired length, ending with a row 3.

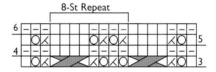

ENDING SECTION

Decrease Row (WS): K3, *p1, p2tog, p1, k4*; repeat from * to * until last 7 stitches, p1, p2tog, p1, k3—37 sts.

Next Row: K1, yo, p2tog, k3 *[p2tog, yo] twice, k3 *; repeat from * to * until last 3 stitches, p2tog, yo, k1.

Bind off all stitches in pattern.

FINISHING

Using the yarn needle, weave in all ends. If desired, very lightly steam block using a steam iron on a wool setting. Don't let the iron come any closer than 3" (7.6 cm) to your knitting. Steam just enough to relax the selvedge edges.

LACE CABLE

Cables can get heavy. Every other row of this cable is worked in a simple lace pattern resulting in a lighter weight and unusual looking cable.

BASIC PATTERN
Multiple of 9 stitches with 4 edge stitches *(optional)*

- ☐ Knit on RS, purl on WS
- ⊟ Purl on RS, knit on WS
- ☒ K2tog in knit stitches; P2tog in purl stitches
- ☑ Yarn Over (yo)
- 9-St RKC

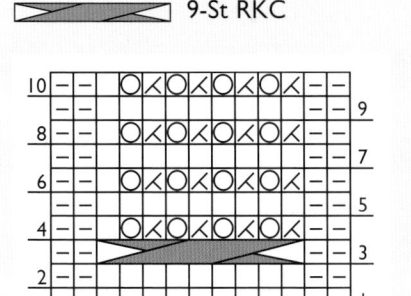

9-St Repeat

Row 1 (RS): P2, k9, p2.
Row 2: K2, p9, k2.
Row 3: P2, 9-St RKC, p2.
Row 4: K2, p1, [yo, p2tog] 4 times, k2.
Row 5: P2, k9, p2.
Row 6: K2, p1, [yo, p2tog] 4 times, k2.
Row 7: P2, k9, p2.
Row 8: K2, p1, [yo, p2tog] 4 times, k2.
Row 9: P2, k9, p2.
Row 10: K2, p1, [yo, p2tog] 4 times, k2.
Repeat rows 1 – 10.

LACE CABLE – MAKE A SWATCH

Cast on 31 stitches.

Row 1 (RS): K2, p3, [k9, p3] twice, k2.
Row 2: K5, p1, [yo, p2tog] 4 times, k3, p9, k5.
Row 3: K2, p3, 9-St RKC, p3, k9, p3, k2.
Row 4: K5, * p1, [yo, p2tog] 4 times, k3*; repeat from * to * to last 2 sts, k2.
Row 5: K2, p3, [k9, p3] twice, k2.
Row 6: K5, p9, k3, p1, [yo, p2tog] 4 times, k5.
Row 7: K2, p3, k9, p3, 9-St RKC, p3, k2.
Row 8: K5, * p1, [yo, p2tog] 4 times, k3*; repeat from * to * to last 2 sts, k2.
Row 9: K2, p3, [k9, p3] twice, k2.
Row 10: K5, * p1, [yo, p2tog] 4 times, k3*; repeat from * to * to last 2 sts, k2.
Rows 11 – 30: Repeat rows 1 – 10 (two more times).
Rows 31 – 35: Repeat rows 1 – 5.
Bind off all stitches in pattern.

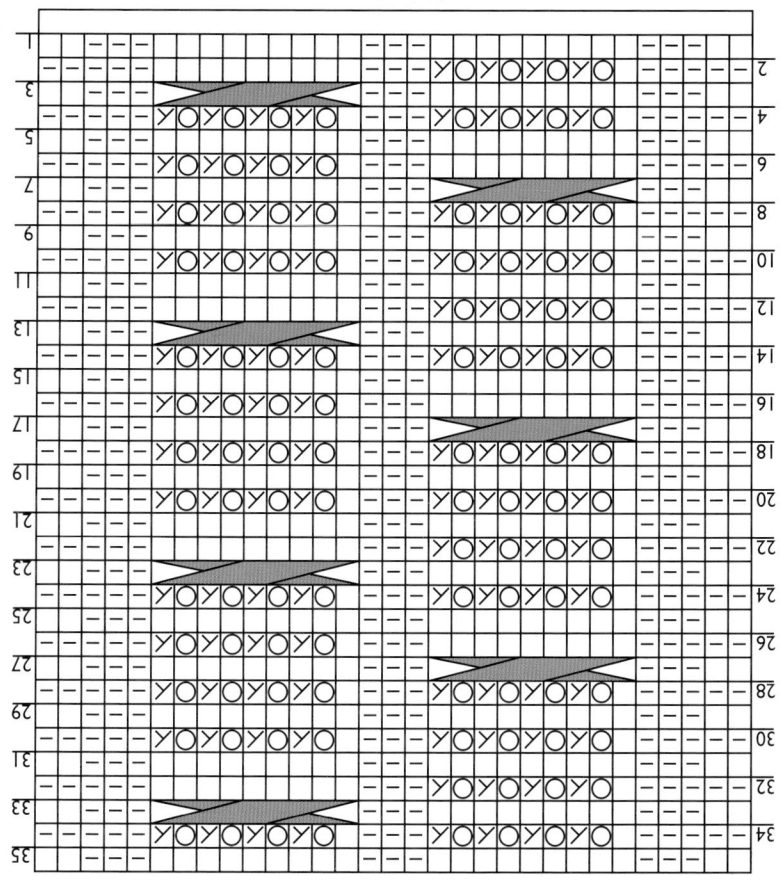

31 Stitches

Legend:

- ☐ Knit on RS, purl on WS
- ☐ Purl on RS, knit on WS
- ☒ K2tog in knit stitches; P2tog in purl stitches
- ⵔ Yarn Over (yo)
- ⬚ 9-St RKC

PINEAPPLES AND VINES CABLE

Seed stitch and Stockinette stitch combine to create a whimsical cable that looks attractive from both sides.

BASIC PATTERN
Multiple of 7 stitches with 4 edge stitches *(optional)*

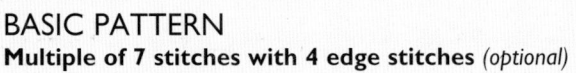

□ Knit on RS, purl on WS
⊟ Purl on RS, knit on WS

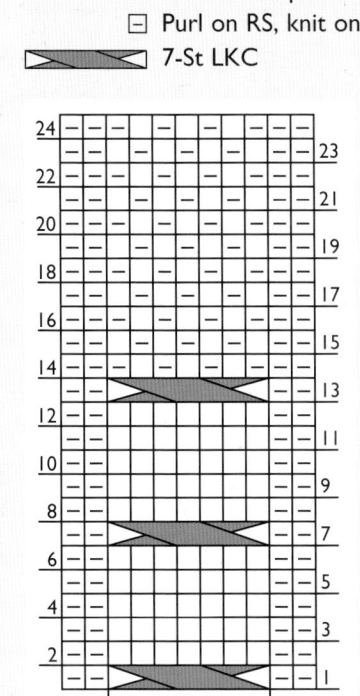

7-St Repeat

Row 1 (RS): P2, 7-St LKC, p2.
Row 2: K2, p7, k2.
Row 3: P2, k7, p2.
Rows 4: K2, p7, k2.
Rows 5: P2, k7, p2.
Row 6: K2, p7, k2.
Rows 7 – 12: Repeat rows 1 – 6.
Row 13: P2, 7-St LKC, p2.
Row 14: K3, [p1, k1] 3 times, k2.
Row 15: P2, k1, [p1, k1] 3 times, p2.
Rows 16 – 23: Repeat rows 14 – 15 (4 more times.)
Row 24: K3, [p1, k1] 3 times, k2.
Repeat rows 1 – 24.

PINEAPPLES AND VINES CABLE SWATCH – MAKE A SWATCH

Cast on 31 stitches.

Row 1 (RS): K1, p1, k7, p3, k1, [p1, k1] 3 times, p3, k7, p1, k1.

Row 2: K2, p7, k4, p1, [k1, p1] twice, k4, p7, k2.

Row 3: K1, p1, k7, p3, k1, [p1, k1] 3 times, p3, k7, p1, k1.

Row 4: K2, p7, k4, p1, [k1, p1] twice, k4, p7, k2.

Row 5: K1, p1, 7-St LKC, p3, k1, [p1, k1] 3 times, p3, 7-St LKC, p1, k1.

Row 6: K2, p7, k4, p1, [k1, p1] twice, k4, p7, k2.

Row 7: K1, p1, k7, p3, k1, [p1, k1] 3 times, p3, k7, p1, k1.

Row 8: K2, p7, k4, p1, [k1, p1] twice, k4, p7, k2.

Row 9: K1, p1, k7, p3, k1, [p1, k1] 3 times, p3, k7, p1, k1.

Row 10: K2, p7, k4, p1, [k1, p1] twice, k4, p7, k2.

Row 11: K1, p1, [7-St LKC, p3] twice, 7-St LKC, p1, k1.

Row 12: K3, p1, [k1, p1] twice, k4, p7, k4, p1, [k1, p1] twice, k3.

Row 13: K1, [p1, k1] 4 times, p3, k7, p3, [k1, p1] 4 times, k1.

Row 14: K3, p1, [k1, p1] twice, k4, p7, k4, p1, [k1, p1] twice, k3.

Row 15: K1, [p1, k1] 4 times, p3, k7, p3, [k1, p1] 4 times, k1.

Row 16: K3, p1, [k1, p1] twice, k4, p7, k4, p1, [k1, p1] twice, k3.

Row 17: K1, [p1, k1] 4 times, p3, 7-St LKC, p3, [k1, p1] 4 times, k1.

Rows 18 – 22: Repeat rows 12 – 16.

Row 23: K1, p1, [7-St LKC, p3] twice, 7-St LKC, p1, k1.

Row 24: K2, p7, k4, p1, [k1, p1] twice, k4, p7, k2.

Rows 25 – 34: Repeat rows 1 – 10.

Bind off all stitches in pattern.

□ Knit on RS, purl on WS

⊟ Purl on RS, knit on WS

7-St LKC

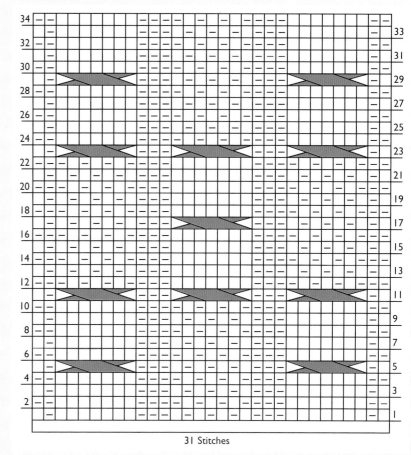

31 Stitches

TWINING VINES CABLE

This cable is often called a Mutton Chop cable. It's much too pretty for that so I've created a new name— Twining Vines. Stockinette stitch and Reverse Stockinette stitch combine to create a lovely feminine texture.

If you want to control the flare at the top, then bind off within a few rows after the cable crossing.

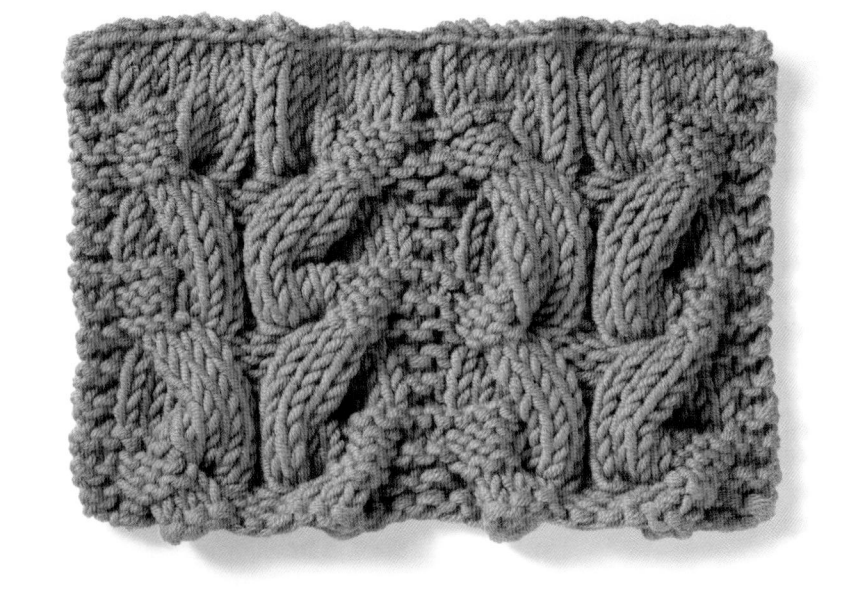

BASIC PATTERN
Multiple of 20 stitches with 2 edge stitches

☐ Knit on RS, purl on WS
⊟ Purl on RS, knit on WS

8-St RPC

8-St LPC

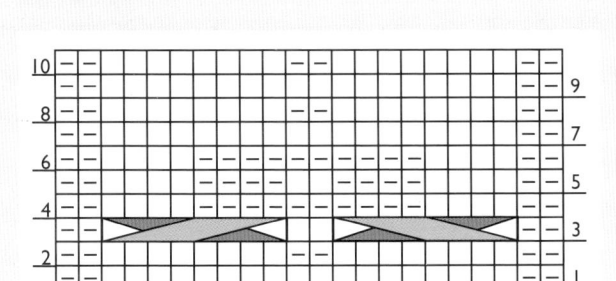

20-St Repeat

Row 1 (RS): P2, k18, p2.
Row 2: K2, [p8, k2] twice.
Row 3: P2, 8-St LPC, k2, 8-St RPC, p2.
Row 4: K2, p4, k10, p4, k2.
Row 5: P2, k4, p4, k2, p4, k4, p2.
Row 6: K2, p4, k10, p4, k2.
Rows 7 – 10: Repeat rows 1 – 2 (two more times).

TWINING VINES CABLE – MAKE A SWATCH

Cast on 42 stitches.

Row 1 (RS): K10, p2, k18, p2, k10.

Row 2: K2, [p8, k2] 4 times.

Row 3: [K2, 8-St RPC, p2, 8-St LPC] twice, k2.

Row 4: K6, p4, k2, p4, k10, p4, k2, p4, k6.

Row 5: [K2, p4, k4, p2, k4, p4] twice, k2.

Row 6: K6, p4, k2, p4, k10, p4, k2, p4, k6.

Row 7: K10, p2, k18, p2, k10.

Row 8: K2, [p8, k2] 4 times.

Row 9: K10, p2, k18, p2, k10.

Row 10: K2, [p8, k2] 4 times.

Rows 11 – 30: Repeat rows 1 – 10 (two more times.)

Bind off all stitches in pattern.

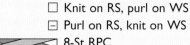

☐ Knit on RS, purl on WS
⊟ Purl on RS, knit on WS
8-St RPC
8-St LPC

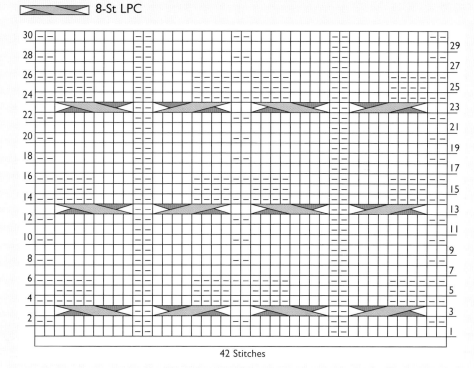

42 Stitches

TWINING VINES NECK WARMER

Winter can stay around as long as it wants when you're wearing this charming neck warmer. The natural tendency of this cable to flare at the edge is used to full advantage, creating a feminine look. Since this will sit right on your neck, be sure and use a very soft yarn. The contrast edge looks just as good worn on the bottom as on the top.

FINISHED MEASUREMENTS
17" circumference x 4¾" height (43.2 x 12.1 cm)

GAUGE
22 stitches and 27 rows = 4" (10 cm) in stockinette stitch
34 stitches and 32 rows = 4" (10 cm) in cable pattern

MATERIALS
Main Color: Light weight yarn, approx 110 yd (100 m)
Contrast Color: Light weight yarn, approx 20 yd (18 m)

THE YARN USED FOR THIS PROJECT
Main Color: Classic Elite Wool Bam Boo; 50% wool, 50% bamboo;
    118 yd (108 m)/1.75 oz (50 g): 1 ball, color Key Lime #1635
Contrast Color: Classic Elite Wool Bam Boo; 50% wool, 50% bamboo;
    118 yd (108 m)/1.75 oz (50 g): 1 ball, color Indigo #1647

NEEDLES AND NOTIONS
Size 6 (4 mm) 24" (61 cm) circular knitting needle or size necessary
    to obtain gauge
Cable needle
Yarn needle for weaving in ends

SETUP ROW

Note: This pattern begins on a wrong side row.

Using Main Color, cast on 142 stitches.

Begin by working one wrong side row.

Set Up Row (WS): K2, * p8, k2 *; repeat from * to * until end of row.

MAIN SECTION

Now the cable is repeated several times until the desired length in the main color is reached. Using Stitch Chart, work as follows:

Row 1 (RS): K10, p2, [k18, p2] 6 times, k10.

Row 2: K2, [p8, k2] 14 times.

Row 3: K2, 8-St RPC, p2, [8-St LPC, k2, 8-St RPC, p2] 6 times, 8-St LPC, k2.

Row 4: K6, p4, [k2, p4, k10, p4] 6 times, k2, p4, k6.

Row 5: K2, p4, k4, p2, [k4, p4, k2, p4, k4, p2] 6 times, k4, p4, k2.

Row 6: K6, p4 [k2, p4, k10, p4] 6 times, k2, p4, k6.

Row 7: K10, p2, [k18, p2] 6 times, k10.

Row 8: K2, [p8, k2] 14 times.

Row 9: K10, p2, [k18, p2] 6 times, k10.

Row 10: K2, [p8, k2] 14 times.

Repeat rows 1 – 10 (3 more times).

Repeat rows 1 – 6 (once)—46 rows.

ENDING ROWS

For the final rows you will change the 2-stitch garter sections to reverse stockinette stitch in order to accentuate the scallop. Also, you will change to the Contrast Color.

Row 1: With Main Color, p2, *k8, p2*; repeat from * to * until end of row. Change to Contrast Color.

Row 2: K2, * p8, k2 *; repeat from * to * until end of row

Row 3: P2, *k8, p2*; repeat from * to * until end of row.

Row 4: K2, *p8, k2*; repeat from * to * until end of row.

Bind off all stitches in pattern.

FINISHING

Seam the two short edges together to create a tube.

Sew invisibly using Main Color.

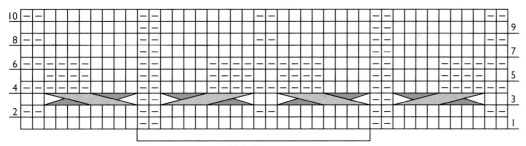

20-St Repeat

REVERSIBLE RIB CABLE

By now you've probably noticed that most cables have a definite right side and wrong side. This cable is created using a rib stitch and both sides are identical.

BASIC PATTERN
Multiple of 8 stitches with 4 edge stitches *(optional)*

☐	Knit on RS, purl on WS
⊟	Purl on RS, knit on WS
▨▨▨	8-St RIB RC

Row 1 (RS): P2, 8-St RIB RC, p2.
Row 2: K2, [k1, p1] 4 times, k2.
Row 3: P2, [k1, p1] 4 times, p2.
Row 4: K2, [k1, p1] 4 times, k2.
Rows 5 – 12: Repeat rows 1 – 4 (two more times).
Rows 13 – 24: Repeat rows 3 – 4 (6 more times).
Repeat rows 1 – 24.

8-St Repeat

REVERSIBLE RIB CABLE – MAKE A SWATCH

Cast on 36 stitches.

Row 1 (RS): K3, *p1, k1*; repeat from * to * until last stitch, k1.

Row 2: K3, *p1, k1*; repeat from * to * until last stitch, k1.

Row 3: K2, *8-St RIB RC, [k1, p1] 4 times*; repeat from * to * until last 2 sts, k2.

Row 4: K3, *p1, k1*; repeat from * to * until last stitch, k1.

Row 5 – 12: Repeat rows 1 – 4 (two more times).

Rows 13: K3, *p1, k1*; repeat from * to * until last stitch, k1.

Rows 14: K3, *p1, k1*; repeat from * to * until last stitch, k1.

Row 15: K2, *[k1, p1] 4 times, 8-St RIB RC*; repeat from * to * until last 2 sts, k2.

Row 16: K3, *p1, k1*; repeat from * to * until last stitch, k1.

Rows 17 – 24: Repeat rows 13 – 16 (two more times).

Rows 25 – 36: Repeat rows 1 – 12.

Row 37: K3, *p1, k1*; repeat from * to * until last stitch, k1.

Bind off all stitches in pattern.

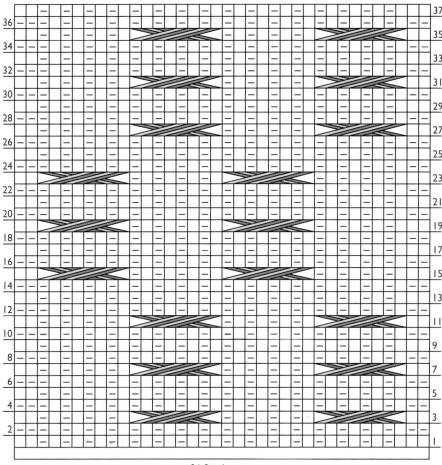

□ Knit on RS, purl on WS

⊟ Purl on RS, knit on WS

8-St RIB RC

36 Stitches

BOHO SUEDE BELT

Channel your inner hippie with this funky belt made from 'suede' yarn. The reversible cable is a perfect choice for this easy belt. Finish it with a whimsical beaded fringe.

FINISHED MEASUREMENTS
2" wide X 40" (5.1 X 101.6 cm) long

GAUGE
19 stitches and 27 rows = 4" (10 cm) in stockinette stitch
36 stitches and 29 rows = 4" (10 cm) in cable pattern

MATERIALS
Medium weight suede yarn, approx 150 yd (137 m)
14 large-hole beads for fringe

THE YARN USED FOR THIS PROJECT
Berroco Suede; 100% nylon; 120 yd (111 m)/1.75 oz (50 g: 2 balls,
    color Palomino #3746

NEEDLES AND NOTIONS
Size 7 (4.5 mm) knitting needles or size necessary to obtain gauge
Cable needle
Floss threaders (available in dental care section of drug store)
Yarn needle for weaving in ends

Note: Adjust the length of the belt to fit your own requirements.
Each 24-row repeat of the cable equals about 3⅓ inches (8.5 cm).
The cable chart was repeated 15 times for the belt shown.

BOHO BELT CHART

☐ Knit on RS, purl on WS
⊟ Purl on RS, knit on WS
▨ 8-St RIB RC

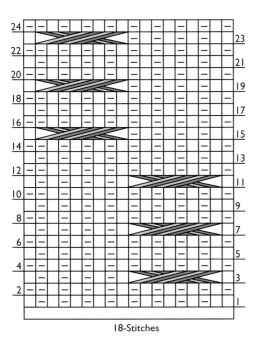

18-Stitches

BELT

Cast on 18 stitches.

Row 1 (RS): K2, * p1, k1 * repeat from * to * until end of row.
Row 2: K2, * p1, k1 * repeat from * to * until end of row.
Row 3: K1, 8-St RIB RC, k1, *p1, k1* repeat from * to * until end of row.
Row 4: K2, * p1, k1 * repeat from * to * until end of row.
Rows 5 – 12: Repeat rows 1 – 4 (two more times).
Row 13 – 14: Repeat rows 1 – 2.
Row 15: K1, [k1, p1] 4 times, 8-St RIB RC, k1.
Row 16: K2, * p1, k1 * repeat from * to * until end of row.
Rows 17 – 24: Repeat rows 13 – 16 (two more times).
Repeat rows 1 – 24 until belt is desired length, ending on Row 12 or 24.
Repeat row 1.
Bind off all stitches in pattern.

FINISHING

Using the yarn needle, weave in all ends.

FRINGE

• Cut 28 pieces of fringe, each 17" (43.2 cm) long.

• Evenly space marks for seven fringes along each short end of the belt.

• Hold two fringe lengths together. Using a crochet hook, pull one end of
  two fringe pieces from the back to the front through the end of the belt.
  Make the ends even.

• Working with one fringe end at a time, thread the yarn through the floss
  threader and then pull through the bead. Repeat for all four ends.

• Even up the ends and slide the bead up to the edge of the belt.

• Repeat to attach seven groups of fringe at each short end of the belt.
  If desired, cut all the fringe sections to the same length.

| # KNOTTED CABLE

This clever cable is created by knitting two stitches off the cable needle in front and then passing it to the back. It's a great building block for the butterfly cable on page 92.

BASIC PATTERN
Multiple of 6 stitches with 4 edge stitches *(optional)*

☐	Knit on RS, purl on WS
⊟	Purl on RS, knit on WS
▰▱▰	6-St RC

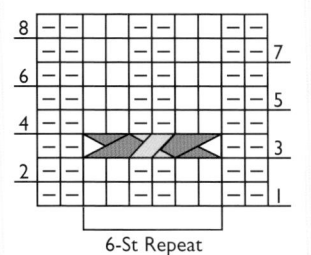

6-St Repeat

Row 1 (RS): P2, k2, p2, k2, p2.
Row 2: K2, p2, k2, p2, k2.
Row 3: P2, 6-St RC, p2.
Row 4: K2, p2, k2, p2, k2.
Rows 5 – 8: Repeat rows 1 –2 (two more times).
Repeat rows 1 – 8.

KNOTTED CABLE – MAKE A SWATCH

Cast on 36 stitches.

Row 1 (RS): K3, p3, [k2, p2, k2, p3] 3 times, k3.

Row 2: K6, [p2, k2, p2, k3] twice, p2, k2, p2, k6.

Row 3: K3, p3, 6-St RC, p3, k2, p2, k2, p3, 6-St RC, p3, k3.

Row 4: K6, [p2, k2, p2, k3] twice, p2, k2, p2, k6.

Rows 5: K3, p3, [k2, p2, k2, p3] 3 times, k3.

Rows 6: K6, [p2, k2, p2, k3] twice, p2, k2, p2, k6.

Row 7: K3, p3, k2, p2, k2, p3, 6-St RC, p3, k2, p2, k2, p3, k3.

Row 8: K6, [p2, k2, p2, k3] twice, p2, k2, p2, k6.

Rows 9 – 24: Repeat rows 1 – 8 (two more times).

Rows 25 – 28: Repeat rows 1 – 4.

Row 29: K3, p3, [k2, p2, k2, p3] 3 times, k3.

Bind off all stitches in pattern.

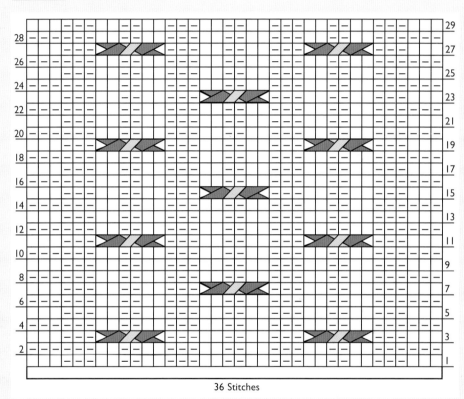

☐ Knit on RS, purl on WS

⊟ Purl on RS, knit on WS

6-St RC

36 Stitches

BUTTERFLY CABLE

This extravagant cable looks like a flight of butterflies when worked in alternating repeats.

BASIC PATTERN
Multiple of 20 stitches with 4 left edge stitches

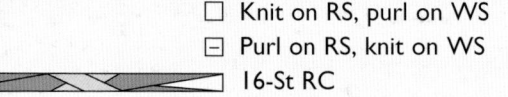

☐ Knit on RS, purl on WS

⊟ Purl on RS, knit on WS

16-St RC

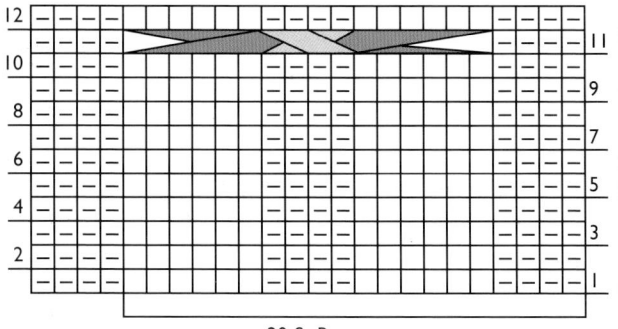

20-St Repeat

Row 1 (RS): P4, [k6, p4] twice.
Row 2: K4, [p6, k4] twice.
Row 3: P4, [k6, p4] twice.
Row 4: K4, [p6, k4] twice.
Row 5: P4, [k6, p4] twice.
Row 6: K4, [p6, k4] twice.
Row 7: P4, [k6, p4] twice.
Row 8: K4, [p6, k4] twice.
Row 9: P4, [k6, p4] twice.
Row 10: K4, [p6, k4] twice.
Row 11: P4, 16-St RC, p4.
Row 12: K4, [p6, k4] twice.

NOTE: You will find this cable easier to work if you place the center four stitches on a 'fish hook' style cable needle (see page 6).

BUTTERFLY CABLE –
MAKE A SWATCH

Cast on 64 stitches.

Row 1 (RS): P4, [k6, p4] 6 times.

Row 2: K4, [p6, k4] 6 times.

Rows 3 – 10: Repeat rows 1 – 2 (4 more times).

Row 11: P4, [16-St RC, p4] 3 times.

Row 12: K4, [p6, k4] 6 times.

Rows 13 – 22: Repeat rows 1 – 2 (5 times).

Row 23: P4, k6, p4, [16-St RC, p4] twice, k6, p4.

Row 24: K4, [p6, k4] 6 times.

Rows 25 – 34: Repeat rows 1 – 2 (5 times).

Rows 35 – 46: Repeat rows 11 – 22.

Bind off all stitches in pattern.

☐ Knit on RS, purl on WS

⊟ Purl on RS, knit on WS

16-St RC

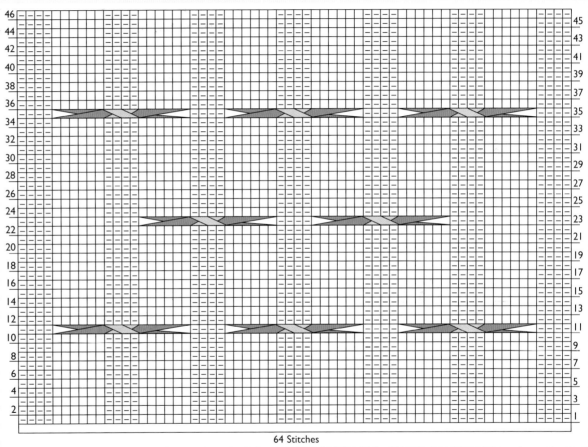

64 Stitches

CASHMERE BUTTERFLY WRAP

Two hand dyed yarns, cashmere and kid mohair, are combined to create a sumptuous wrap that is just as soft as it is pretty. The two strands are worked together and you'll be surprised by how quick and easy it is to create this beautiful design.

FINISHED MEASUREMENTS
19" wide × 40" long (48.3 × 101.6 cm)

GAUGE
14 stitches and 20 rows = 4" (10 cm) in stockinette stitch
26 stitches and 25 rows = 4" (10 cm) in cable pattern

MATERIALS
Yarn A: Variegated, fingering weight cashmere, approx 800 yd (732 m)
Yarn B: Variegated, light weight kid mohair, approx 800 yd (732 m)

THE YARN USED FOR THIS PROJECT
Yarn A: Jade Sapphire 2 ply Mongolian Cashmere; 100% cashmere;
    400 yd (366 m)/2 oz (55 g): 2 hanks color Plum Rose #024
Yarn B: Colinette Parisienne; 70% kid mohair, 30% polymide; 242 yd
    (221 m)/0.875 oz (25 g): 4 hanks, color Florentina

NEEDLES AND NOTIONS
Size 10½ (6.5 mm) knitting needles or size necessary to obtain gauge
Two cable needles (preferably, one fish-hook style)
Yarn needle for weaving in ends

For ease in working with a large number of stitches, use longer needles
or a circular needle.

WRAP

With one strand of Yarn A and Yarn B held
together, cast on 124 stitches.

Row 1 (RS): P4, *k6, p4 *; repeat from * to *
until end of row.

Row 2: K4, *p6, k4*; repeat from * to *
until end of row.

Rows 3 – 10: Repeat rows 1 – 2 (4 more times).

Row 11: P4, *16-St RC, p4 *; repeat from * to *
until end of row.

Row 12: K4, *p6, k4*; repeat from * to *
until end of row.

Rows 13 – 22: Repeat rows 1 – 2 (5 times).

Row 23: P4, k6, p4, [16-St RC, p4] 5 times, k6, p4.

Row 24: K4, *p6, k4*; repeat from * to *
until end of row.

Repeat rows 1 – 24 (9 times more).

Repeat rows 1 – 22 (once).

Bind off all stitches in pattern.

FINISHING

Using the yarn needle, weave in all ends.

If desired, very lightly steam block using a steam
iron on a wool setting. Don't let the iron come any
closer than 3" (7.6 cm) to your knitting.

Steam just enough to relax the selvedge edges.

BUTTERFLY WRAP CHART

Note: This pattern is worked throughout with one strand of Yarn A and Yarn B held together.

☐ Knit on RS, purl on WS

⊟ Purl on RS, knit on WS

16-St RC

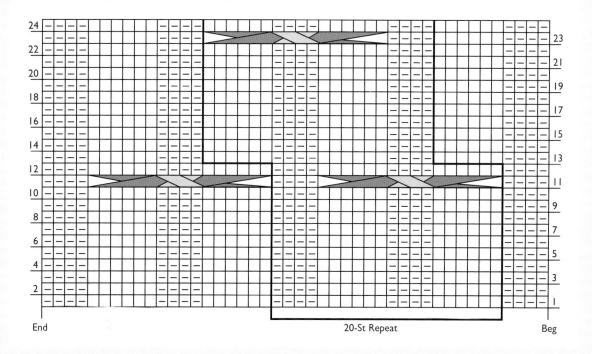

End   20-St Repeat   Beg

The middle section of 20 stitches, marked with heavy lines, is repeated until the desired width is reached. The sections outside the heavy lines are used only once to complete the side edges. If you want to change the width of your wrap, then add or decrease the number of stitches by multiples of 20 stitches.

KNITTING ABBREVIATIONS

cm	centimeters
dec	decrease
g	grams
k	knit
inc	knit into front and back loop of same stitch or purl into front and back loop of same stitch
k2tog	knit two stitches together
MB	make bobble

M1	increase 1 by inserting the left hand needle under the horizontal thread between the stitch just worked and the next st; knit into the back of the resulting loop to make a stitch
mm	millimeters
p	purl
p2tog	purl two stitches together

psso	pass slipped st over
RS	right side
sl	slip
ssk	slip the first and second stitches one at a time kwise, then insert left hand needle into the fronts of these stitches and knit them together.
st(s)	stitch(es)

St st	Stockinette stitch (k on RS, p on WS)
WS	wrong side
yo	yarn over needle
*	repeat instructions between * as directed
[ ]	repeat instructions enclosed by brackets as directed

INDEX